T0312361

Gennaro's
CUCINA

Gennaro's
CUCINA

HEARTY MONEY-SAVING MEALS FROM AN ITALIAN KITCHEN

PHOTOGRAPHY BY DAVID LOFTUS

PAVILION

CONTENTS

INTRODUCTION

Cucina povera is the basis from which all our favourite Italian dishes come from. It's the sort of cooking I was brought up on and still cook today. It originates mainly from rural areas, where meals were created using the limited number of ingredients available – either what people grew or what little they could afford to buy. In doing so, they learnt to value what they had and to lovingly cook dishes to ensure they tasted better, using all their imagination to make dishes go as far as they could.

The seasons played an important part, bringing an abundance of particular produce at certain times of the year in different regions of the country. Therefore, people had to find creative ways to cook the produce, so that a surplus would never be wasted and instead was preserved to enjoy at other times of the year. This is how salting fish or curing meats came about, hence the abundance of cured meats in Italian delis today. A glut of vegetables would be preserved in oil, and the end-of-summer tomatoes placed in glass bottles or fruit drying in the sun were familiar, annual rituals for most Italian families.

Pasta, simply made with flour and water, forms a huge part of the rustic Italian kitchen. Shapes such as *orecchiette* from Puglia or *trofie* in Liguria form the basis of many delicious regional dishes, which over time have become renowned outside of Italy, too. Pasta was traditionally the main staple of the south, whereas in the north, rice and polenta were eaten more readily. This is where risotto and the delicious gooey and baked polenta dishes stem from.

Bread, which we often take for granted these days, as toast for breakfast or a quick sandwich at lunchtime, has always been an important food in Italy. No Italian meal would be complete without bread on the table, but it is also put to good use in recipes. Stale bread is never wasted – think of Tuscan *Panzanella* Salad, drizzled with olive oil and combined with tomatoes and olives. In Puglia, a dish called *Panecotto* is very popular and comprises stale bread cooked in a broth, perhaps with the addition of vegetables. Many soups are made with bread – Tuscan *Ribollita* or *Pappa al Pomodoro* to name just two – each region having its own version.

Bread is also used as a filling to stuff vegetables or added to meatballs to replace some of the meat. In Sicily, breadcrumbs are used to sprinkle over pasta, often in place of cheese.

Whenever I have stale bread, I make breadcrumbs, which I then store in containers to use for coating meat or fish or sprinkling on baked dishes or pasta. Bread dough was never wasted either; pizza makers in Naples would fry scraps of dough, which were topped with tomato sauce and cheese, and known locally as *Diavulilli* or *Angiolilli*.

Throughout Italy, recipes often include the name *Scappati* or *Fuggiti*, meaning 'escaped' – the escape refers to a particular meat or fish which has magically 'escaped', because it wasn't there in the first place as it was probably too expensive to buy.

In Naples, when you couldn't afford the clams for *Spaghetti alle Vongole*, all the other ingredients were added, but they said the vongole had 'escaped'! There is also a recipe from Castellamare di Stabia for seafood pasta, called *Pasta con i Sassi*, which uses pebbles from the sea to flavour the pasta water – I can only assume and hope the pebbles were removed before serving!

Cheaper cuts of meat and offal were often used to create wonderful dishes – think of slow-cooked ragùs and stews made with these. Offal was often sold very cheaply or even given away by butchers who sold meat to the rich. The offal would be made into dishes like the spicy *Neapolitan Soffritto* made with lots of herbs and chilli to mask the flavour; *Trippa* (tripe) was made into various dishes all over Italy; also *Fegato alla Veneziana* – liver cooked with lots of onions, from Venice. No part of the animal was ever wasted and even pig's blood was used to make chocolate. A lot of these dishes still exist today and have also become gourmet delicacies.

Fish was often dried and salted so it could be kept for long periods. *Baccalà* (salt cod) or *Stoccafisso* (air-dried cod) are both prime examples of how this food of the poor has become so popular and now commands such high prices. It has now become the food of the rich, and it is a treat to enjoy this cured fish, especially at Christmastime. *Baccalà* is eaten throughout the regions of Italy in a variety of ways. In Venice, it is cooked in milk, then reduced to a mushy consistency with olive oil and garlic and served on grilled polenta. In Liguria, it is cooked with potatoes, and in Naples, it is cooked in a tomato sauce.

Beans and pulses are widely used in Italian cooking and this probably dates back to when meat prices were so prohibitive. Italians love thick, bean-based soups and pasta dishes, and each region has its own specialities, made using whatever beans or pulses are locally grown, along with other ingredients that are popular in that particular area. Beans and pulses are a great source of protein, they are economical and can be used to create some truly lovely meals.

The sheer simplicity and deliciousness of these humble dishes never ceases to amaze me and they give such a great insight into the resourcefulness of the once-poor people of Italy. In recent years, this type of cooking has become very fashionable and can now be enjoyed in some of the best restaurants, often commanding high prices. For these dishes to be cooked at home, as well as in top restaurants, surely indicates that the poor Italians of years ago actually ate very well!

I hope you will enjoy and recreate some of my favourite Italian rustic dishes in this book – including some from my home region of Campania, as well as recipes from northern and central Italy and the islands. Each recipe tells a story and together they all form the rich tapestry that makes up the food culture of my beloved country. I have tried to make the recipes as simple as possible with easily obtainable ingredients; some recipes take a little time, but most are quick and easy for even the most amateur cook to recreate.

Buon Appetito!

RICE, POLENTA AND GRAINS

CHISCIOL

Cheesy buckwheat pancakes

This ancient *cucina povera* recipe, from the Alpine region of La Valtellina in northern Italy traditionally uses the local ingredients of buckwheat, grappa and Casera cheese. I've replaced the grappa with white wine, but if you have this strong liqueur then do use it. For the cheese, I've used Gruyère, but you could use Comté or a strong, mature Cheddar. For best results, use a heavy-based pan so you get a nice crispy bottom and a soft inside oozing with melted cheese. Serve one pancake per person along with a mixed salad for a nutritious meal. Buckwheat is packed full of nutrients and it's gluten-free (although the pasta flour in this recipe isn't gluten-free).

Makes 4 large filled pancakes
150g (5½oz) buckwheat flour
100g (3½oz) '00' pasta flour
pinch of sea salt
50ml (2fl oz) white wine
350ml (12fl oz) water
butter, for greasing
200g (8½oz) Gruyère cheese, thinly sliced

Sift the flours and salt into a bowl, whisk in the wine, then gradually whisk in the water until you have a lump-free batter that is not too liquid. Cover and leave to rest for 10 minutes.

Heat a small, heavy-based frying or pancake pan (about 20cm/8in. in diameter) over a medium-to-high heat, then when it's hot, grease with a little butter. Add a ladleful of the batter, cook for about 30 seconds, then place a few slices of cheese on top. Add another ladleful of batter and continue to cook for a minute or so until golden underneath. With the help of a fish slice, carefully flip the pancake over and continue to cook for 2–3 minutes, until the bottom has formed a golden crust and the cheese has melted nicely.

Transfer the pancake to a plate and keep warm while you repeat with the remaining batter and cheese to make four pancakes in total. Serve hot.

TIMBALLO DI RISO

Risotto bake

Risotto is a typical staple of northern Italy. However, *Timballo di Riso*, also known as *Sartù*, is a traditional Neapolitan dish that dates back to the 1700s. At this time, rice was considered a poor and insipid food and so the Neapolitan royal cooks set out to enrich it by adding meat, cheese and vegetables and creating a substantial baked dish to satisfy the king. It worked and, over time, it has become a great recipe to use up leftovers – ragù, vegetables, cheese, ham, cured meats, and anything else you like. And even leftover risotto rice can be used – simply mix with a béchamel or tomato sauce and some grated cheese and bake.

This is my version of a *Sartù Napoletano*, but, you can use pretty much any ingredients you like. You can bake it in an ovenproof dish or, if you dare, try a cake tin so you can serve it like a cake. However, if you do this, ensure you have a loose-bottomed tin and grease it well. Be warned, this is a very substantial meal. Buon Appetito!

Serves 4–6

2 tbsp extra virgin olive oil
1 small onion, finely chopped
½ celery stick, finely chopped
1 small carrot, finely chopped
200g (7oz) beef mince
2 tbsp (30ml/1fl oz) white wine
1 x 400g (14oz) can chopped tomatoes,
    blended until smooth, or use 400g (14oz)
    tomato passata
250g (9oz) risotto rice
approx. 780ml (27fl oz) hot vegetable stock
100g (3½oz) frozen peas
25g (1oz) butter, plus extra for

greasing and dotting
35g (1¼oz) grated Parmesan cheese
1 tbsp dried breadcrumbs, plus extra
    for coating
1 x 125g/4½oz ball of mozzarella cheese,
    drained and roughly chopped
1 egg, lightly beaten

For the béchamel sauce
20g (¾oz) butter
20g (¾oz) plain flour
250ml (generous 1 cup) milk
sea salt and freshly ground black pepper

Heat the olive oil in a large saucepan, add the onion, celery and carrot and sweat over a medium heat for about 5 minutes until softened. Stir in the beef mince and cook until well sealed, about 7 minutes. Add the white wine and cook until it has evaporated. Add the tomatoes or tomato passata, cover with a lid, then reduce the heat and cook for 40 minutes.

Stir in the rice, add a ladleful of hot stock and cook over a medium heat, stirring with a wooden spoon, until the liquid has been absorbed. Continue adding the hot stock like this, a ladleful at a time, cooking and stirring for about 17 minutes until the risotto is cooked to al dente and all the stock has been absorbed. About 5 minutes before the end

of the cooking time, stir in the peas. Remove from the heat and stir in the butter and half of the grated Parmesan. Leave to cool.

Preheat the oven to 180°C fan/200°C/gas mark 6. Grease a deep 25.5 x 13cm (10in.) spherical cake tin (approximately 21cm in diameter) or a similar ovenproof dish with some butter, then sprinkle with the breadcrumbs to coat, tapping out the excess.

While the oven is heating, make the béchamel sauce. Melt the butter in a small saucepan, remove from the heat and whisk in the flour, then gradually whisk in the milk. Return the pan to a medium heat and cook until the sauce thickens slightly, stirring continuously. Remove from the heat and season with a little salt and pepper.

Stir the mozzarella, egg and half of the béchamel sauce into the risotto mixture.

Pour the risotto mixture evenly into the prepared cake tin or ovenproof dish and top with the remaining béchamel sauce. Combine the remaining 1 tablespoon of breadcrumbs with the remaining grated Parmesan, sprinkle over the top of the sauce and dot with butter.

Bake in the oven for 30 minutes until the rice is cooked and a nice golden crust has formed on the top. Remove from the oven, leave to rest for about 5 minutes, then serve.

MESCIUA

Ligurian spelt and bean soup

Spelt is an ancient grain that is used in this thick Ligurian soup, a dish said to date back to the 14th century and that forms part of this northern region's *cucina povera*. The spelt, which is rich in protein, is further enriched with other beans and pulses for a nutritious and hearty meal. Although traditionally made with dried pulses, which need to soak overnight and take longer to cook, in my version I have used the canned variety that work just as well and make it very quick to cook and prepare.

Serves 4
120g (4¼oz) pearled spelt
1 x 400g (14oz) can chickpeas
1 x 400g (14oz) can cannellini beans
1 rosemary sprig
2 tbsp extra virgin olive oil, plus extra for drizzling
1 onion, finely chopped
handful of flat-leaf parsley, finely chopped
1 tsp tomato purée, diluted in a little warm water
sea salt and freshly ground black pepper
rustic bread slices, toasted, to serve

Rinse the spelt under cold running water, then place in a saucepan with plenty of fresh water, bring to the boil and simmer for about 20 minutes until cooked (check the cooking time on your packet).

Meanwhile, place the chickpeas and cannellini beans, including their liquid, in another saucepan with the rosemary and heat through gently.

Heat the olive oil in a small frying pan, add the onion and half of the parsley. Sweat over a low heat for about 5 minutes until softened.

Drain the spelt and add to the chickpeas and cannellini beans, then stir in the tomato purée, followed by the onion mixture and season with some salt and pepper. Discard the rosemary stalk. Serve with a drizzle of olive oil, the rest of the parsley and slices of toasted rustic bread.

POLENTA CONCIA AL FORNO

Cheesy baked polenta

Polenta has always been the staple of northern Italy and, in rural communities, this corn-based flour was often the only food available. Naturally times have changed, but polenta remains a classic and popular dish, especially in the northern mountain areas, where a steaming plate of polenta is always a welcome dish during the winter. *Polenta Concia* is the name given to polenta that is mixed with cheese. You can eat this as soon as the polenta is ready, or, to make it even tastier and to enjoy a crusty top, *Polenta Concia* is delicious baked in the oven. To add more flavour when cooking the polenta, I like to add a couple of vegetable stock pots (each 28g/1oz) to the water, but you can simply use plain water and season later with a little salt, if you prefer.

This is a hearty dish that you can enjoy as a main meal or serve as a side dish with stews. It's also a great way of using up leftover cheese – below are examples of cheese I like to add, but you can use whatever you have to hand. When I tested this recipe, I used Parmesan, Cheddar and Gouda as these were the cheeses I had in my fridge.

Serves 4–6

40g (1½oz) butter
1.2 litres (2 pints) vegetable stock or water
300g (10½oz) quick-cook polenta
320g (11½oz) mixed cheeses, such as
  Parmesan, pecorino, fontina, Cheddar,
Gouda, Gruyère, Gorgonzola, grated or
  cut into very small cubes
4 sage leaves
sea salt (optional)

Preheat the oven to 180°C fan/200°C/gas mark 6. Grease an ovenproof dish with a little of the butter.

Make the polenta. Pour the stock or water into a large saucepan and bring to the boil over a medium heat. Gradually whisk in the polenta, mixing well to avoid lumps forming, then cook, stirring, for about 3–5 minutes (or according to the timing given on the packet) until well combined and creamy. Remove from the heat and beat in half of the mixed cheeses. Season with a little salt if necessary (if using plain water instead of stock).

Pour half of the polenta mixture evenly into the ovenproof dish, scatter with the remaining mixed cheeses, then cover with the remaining polenta. Melt the remaining butter with the sage leaves in a small frying pan over a low-to-medium heat and then pour this over the top of the polenta.

Bake in the oven for about 20 minutes until golden. Remove from the oven and serve immediately.

CALZAGATTI

Polenta and beans

This traditional rural dish from Modena in Emilia Romagna has a funny story about how it came to have the name *Calzagatti*. A lady was making polenta and beans separately, and while bringing both to the table, she tripped over the cat and, as a result, the beans fell into the polenta. I really don't know how true this is, but polenta and beans make a very nutritious dish. I used dried beans, but you can also use the canned variety. This dish can be cooked and served in three different ways – as a gooey polenta, or in slices that can either be fried or grilled. All three are delicious, but my favourite has to be the fried slices.

Serves 4

200g dried borlotti beans, soaked overnight in plenty of cold water, or use 2 x 400g (14oz) cans borlotti beans
4 tbsp extra virgin olive oil, plus (optional) extra for frying
2 garlic cloves, lightly crushed and left whole
60g (2¼oz) pancetta, cubed
2 small rosemary sprigs
800ml (28fl oz) reserved cooking bean water (or plain water mixed with the liquid from the cans of beans, if using canned beans)
200g (7oz) quick-cook polenta
20g (¾oz) grated Parmesan cheese
sea salt and freshly ground black pepper,

Drain and rinse the soaked borlotti beans, then place in a saucepan with plenty of fresh cold water. Bring to the boil and cook until tender, about 40 minutes – check the cooking time on your bean packet. Drain, reserving the cooking water. Set aside.

Heat the olive oil in a frying pan, add the garlic and sweat over a medium heat for a minute or so, then add the pancetta and stir-fry over a medium heat until the pancetta is golden, about 5 minutes. Stir in the cooked (or canned) beans and the rosemary sprigs, add a little salt and pepper to taste and cook for a few minutes until heated through. Remove from the heat and discard the garlic cloves. Set aside.

To make the polenta, pour the (measured) bean water (or measured plain water combined with the bean liquid, if using canned beans) into a saucepan and bring to the boil, then gradually whisk in the polenta, mixing well to prevent lumps forming. Cook, stirring, for about 3–5 minutes or according to the timing given on the packet. Remove the pan from the heat, then stir in the grated Parmesan and the bean mixture (discard the rosemary stalks).

You can now eat it as it is, or pour the mixture into a 2 litre (3½ pint) loaf tin lined with clingfilm and leave to cool and set for about an hour or until required. Once set, tip the polenta out of the loaf tin and cut into 2.5cm (1in.) slices. You can either fry the slices in a little olive oil in a frying pan over a high heat for about 2 minutes on each side, or preheat the grill to high and grill the slices for a couple of minutes on each side until golden brown and nice and crispy. Serve hot.

RISO E LENTICCHIE

Rice and lentils

This nutritious gluten-free dish is simple to prepare and the ultimate comfort food. If you're vegetarian, simply omit the pancetta and ensure the cheese you use (pecorino or Parmesan) is suitable for vegetarians. If you don't have celery, don't worry, use carrot instead, and if you don't have fresh tomatoes, simply use a couple of canned plum ones. If you prefer, you can also use grated Parmesan instead of pecorino or a drizzle of extra virgin olive oil. I'm sure this easy mid-week meal will soon become a popular choice.

Serves 2–4
250g (9oz) dried small brown or green
  lentils, such as Puy or Castelluccio
2 tbsp extra virgin olive oil
50g (1¾oz) pancetta, finely chopped
1 onion, finely chopped
1 celery stick, finely chopped
1 garlic clove, lightly crushed and left whole
2 ripe tomatoes, finely chopped
1.7 litres (3 pints) vegetable stock
250g (9oz) arborio rice (not rinsed)
handful of flat-leaf parsley, finely chopped
20g (¾oz) grated pecorino cheese

Check your packet of lentils as they may need pre-soaking. If so, leave to soak overnight in plenty of cold water, then drain and rinse well; if not, rinse them well in plenty of cold water.

Heat the olive oil in a large saucepan, add the pancetta and onion and sweat over a medium heat for about 3 minutes until softened. Stir in the celery, garlic and tomatoes and continue to cook for a minute or so.

Add the stock and lentils, bring to the boil, then reduce the heat and simmer gently – check your packet of lentils for the recommended cooking time. Halfway through the cooking time, stir in the rice and then continue to simmer, uncovered, until the rice and lentils are cooked. This will take about 35 minutes in total, depending on the type of lentils used. Once ready, the lentils should be tender and the rice al dente. The consistency should be dense; in between a thick soup and a risotto.

Remove from the heat and stir in the parsley and pecorino, then serve immediately.

INSALATA DI FARRO

Spelt salad

This ancient grain is making a comeback and creates a lovely salad with the addition of some vegetables and cheese. Packed full of nutrients, it makes a lovely main course or side dish. It tastes even better if made in advance and served the next day. Remember to serve at room temperature and add a drizzle of extra virgin olive oil just before serving.

Serves 2–4 (2 as a main course; 4 as a side dish)
120g (4¼oz) pearled spelt
50g (1¾oz) trimmed green beans
100g (3½oz) broccoli florets
50g (1¾oz) deseeded yellow pepper,
  finely sliced
80g (3oz) baby plum tomatoes, cut in half
2 tbsp extra virgin olive oil, plus extra
  for drizzling
85g (3oz) provolone cheese, cut into
  small cubes
zest of ½ lemon
sea salt and freshly ground black pepper

Rinse the spelt under cold running water, then place in a saucepan with plenty of fresh water, bring to the boil and simmer for about 20 minutes until cooked and tender (check the cooking time on your packet). Drain, rinse under cold running water, then again and leave to cool.

In the meantime, cook the green beans and broccoli in a separate pan of boiling water for about 5 minutes until just tender, then drain well and leave to cool.

Place the green beans, broccoli, yellow pepper and tomatoes in a serving bowl and toss together well with the olive oil and a little salt and pepper. Stir in the cooked spelt, the provolone and lemon zest and then drizzle with some more olive oil.

Serve immediately or cover and store in the fridge for up to 3 days until required, then serve at room temperature with an extra drizzle of olive oil.

RISOTTO ALLA ZUCCA
Pumpkin risotto

Pumpkin risotto is one of my favourite comfort foods and it's perfect during the cooler months when squash is in season and plentiful. This *cucina povera* dish originates from the rural areas of northern Italy where pumpkins used to grow in abundance and rice was a staple. Go for the green, thick-skinned pumpkin if you can, but the more widely available butternut squash is just as good. I like to add a little chilli to this dish to give it a bit of a kick, but that's entirely up to you.

Serves 4

4 tbsp extra virgin olive oil, plus extra for drizzling
1 leek, finely chopped
2 rosemary sprigs, needles stripped and finely
  chopped
½ red chilli, finely chopped (optional)
450g (1lb) pumpkin flesh (peeled and deseeded
  weight), cut into small chunks
300g (10½oz) arborio rice
100ml (3½fl oz) white wine
approx. 1.5 litres (2¾ pints) hot vegetable stock
40g (1½oz) grated Parmesan cheese, plus (optional)
  extra for serving

Heat the olive oil in a large, heavy-based saucepan, add the leek and sweat over a medium heat for a couple of minutes, then stir in the rosemary and chilli (if using) and continue to sweat for a minute. Stir in the pumpkin flesh and cook for a minute or so. Stir in the rice, making sure each grain is coated in oil.

Add the wine and cook over a low-to-medium heat until the rice has absorbed it. Add a couple of ladlefuls of the hot stock, stirring with a wooden spoon until the rice has absorbed it all. Add another ladleful or so of stock and stir until absorbed, then continue in this way, cooking and stirring and adding more stock for about 17 minutes, until the risotto is cooked to al dente.

Remove the pan from the heat, add the Parmesan and mix well with a wooden spoon. Serve immediately with a drizzle of olive oil and an extra sprinkling of grated Parmesan, if desired.

GNOCCHI ALLA ROMANA

Baked semolina gnocchi

This traditional rustic Roman dish pre-dates the classic potato gnocchi and comes from a time when potatoes were not yet introduced in Italy and semolina was used to make dumplings like these. Made with a few simple but nutritious ingredients, it is popular all over Italy, and with all its buttery and cheesy goodness, it makes a delicious and satisfying main course, which I'm sure will become a family favourite. You can prepare the dough and assemble it in advance, store in the fridge and bake when required. For a more formal meal, use individual ovenproof dishes that you can serve at the table.

Serves 4–6
1 litre (1¾ pints) milk
80g (3oz) butter, plus extra for greasing
7g (⅛oz) sea salt
pinch of grated nutmeg
250g (9oz) semolina
2 egg yolks
100g (3½oz) grated Parmesan cheese
40g (1½oz) grated pecorino cheese

Place the milk, 30g (1oz) of the butter, the salt and nutmeg in a non-stick saucepan and bring to the boil over a medium heat. Gradually whisk in the semolina until it's all well incorporated and there are no lumps, then continue to beat with a wooden spoon and cook over a low heat for about 5 minutes, until the mixture is thick and begins to pull away from the sides of the pan. Remove from the heat, then stir in the egg yolks and grated Parmesan.

Place a large sheet of baking paper on a work surface, pour the mixture onto it and spread it out to about 1cm (½in.) thick using a wet spatula. Leave to cool and set.

Preheat the oven to 180°C fan/200°C/gas mark 6. Grease an ovenproof dish with butter.

Using a 5cm (2in.) round pastry cutter, cut out round discs of the cooled semolina mixture. Arrange the semolina discs in a single layer in the prepared ovenproof dish, so they are slightly overlapping. Melt the remaining butter, then pour it over the gnocchi and sprinkle with the grated pecorino.

Bake in the oven for 20–25 minutes until golden. Remove from the oven and serve immediately.

FARINELLA

Barley and chickpea fritters

Farinella has ancient roots linked to rural life in the region of Puglia, when farmers often had to make do with whatever flours they had. Often barley was the only grain available and with this they made bread, polenta, biscuits and pastry, as well as sprinkling the flour over vegetables and sauces in order to enrich the dish. Over time, chickpeas were introduced to Italy and so chickpea flour was added to the barley flour, giving more nutrients and also a nuttier flavour.

Farinella was often cooked in a broth made with local wild herbs and turned into a polenta-type consistency. Whatever was left over would be left to harden overnight, cut into small pieces and cooked over the grill in a similar way to polenta.

This is my version of using *Farinella* to make fritters that can be used instead of bread and enjoyed with cured meats and cheese.

Makes 8–10 farinella fritters
100g (3½oz) barley flour
100g (3½oz) chickpea (gram) flour
pinch of sea salt
600ml (1 pint) water
abundant vegetable oil, for frying, plus a little
  for greasing
2 rosemary sprigs, needles stripped, for sprinkling
a selection of cured meats and cheese, to serve

Combine the flours and salt in a saucepan, then gradually whisk in the water until you have no lumps. Place the saucepan over a medium heat and whisk until thickened, about 5 minutes. Remove from the heat and pour into a lightly oiled flat tray, flattening the mixture out evenly with the help of a spatula to about 1cm (0.3in.) thickness, then leave to cool.

Once cooled, cut out 8–10 round shapes using a 8cm (3in.) round pastry or biscuit cutter.

Heat plenty of oil in a large, deep frying pan until hot, then add the *Farinella* and deep-fry for about 3 minutes on each side until golden (you may need to do this in a couple of batches, depending on the size of your pan). Remove and drain on kitchen paper.

These are delicious served hot or cold with a sprinkling of rosemary needles and a selection of cured meats and cheese.

BEANS AND PULSES

RIBOLLITA
Tuscan bean and bread soup

This traditional hearty Tuscan soup is perfect for using up vegetables and stale bread. It was born out of a necessity to make meals go further and last longer, hence the addition of bread. It was probably also made to be eaten for several days, hence its name *Ribollita*, which literally means 'to reboil', as the soup is kept and cooked again for the next meal. However, as with all *cucina povera* dishes, the trick of adding bread to the soup and leaving it to soak gives this dish extra depth and flavour, making it not only wholesome but super tasty.

You can use any type of cabbage, spring greens and spinach and basically any vegetables you have lying around. I have made this version in the traditional way; using dried beans and blending half of the beans with the stock, thereby resulting in a very thick soup, which you can eat with a fork! It does take a little time and planning to prepare, but is so worth it, plus you can make it in advance and keep it in the fridge to reheat for at least a couple of meals.

Serves 4–6

300g (10½oz) dried cannellini beans, soaked overnight in plenty of cold water

2 tbsp extra virgin olive oil, plus extra for drizzling

1 garlic clove, lightly crushed and left whole

1 rosemary sprig

1.7 litres (3 pints) vegetable stock, plus extra if necessary

1 onion, finely chopped

1 celery stick, finely chopped

1 carrot, finely chopped

200g (7oz) ripe plum tomatoes, peeled and deseeded, or use canned tomatoes, roughly chopped

1 large potato, chopped into small cubes

200g (7oz) cabbage, roughly chopped

200g (7oz) cavolo nero, roughly chopped

200g (7oz) Swiss chard, roughly chopped

200g (7oz) stale bread, cut into slices

dried chilli flakes, to serve

Drain and rinse the soaked cannellini beans. Heat 1 tablespoon of olive oil in a large saucepan and sweat the garlic and rosemary over a medium heat for about a minute. Stir in the beans, add the stock, bring to the boil, then reduce the heat and cook, partially covered, for about 50 minutes or until the beans are cooked and tender. Check the cooking instructions on your bean packet.

When the beans are cooked, remove the pan from the heat and, with a slotted spoon, take out about half the beans and set them aside. When the rest of the beans and stock are cool, discard the rosemary stalk and then blend the mixture until smooth, using a handheld stick blender. Set aside.

Heat the remaining 1 tablespoon of olive oil in a separate large saucepan, add the onion, celery and carrot and sweat over a medium heat for about 3 minutes until softened. Stir in

the tomatoes and potato and continue to cook for a couple of minutes. Stir in the cabbage, cavolo nero and Swiss chard and cook for a minute or so until all the leaves wilt a bit. Add the blended bean mixture, cover with a lid and cook over a low heat for about 45 minutes until, the cavolo nero is cooked. Add a little more water or stock, if necessary. Stir in the reserved whole cooked beans and then remove the pan from the heat.

Take a large bowl, line it with a couple of bread slices and top with ladlefuls of the thick soup mixture, then continue making layers like this until you have used all the bread, finishing up with the remaining soup mixture. Cover with clingfilm and leave to cool, then place in the fridge for a few hours, ideally overnight, so all the flavours infuse and the bread soaks up the soup.

When you are ready to serve, tip all the contents into a large saucepan and gently heat through. Divide between individual bowls and serve with a sprinkling of chilli flakes and a drizzle of olive oil.

PANELLE

Sicilian chickpea fritters

Made with only a handful of ingredients, *Panelle* originated from Sicilian *cucina povera*, and the chickpea flour is almost certainly a legacy from the Arab invasions of the island. Over time, these delicious chickpea fritters have become a popular street food, especially in the city of Palermo where *Panellari* can be spotted frying them on most street corners. Typically served in a bread roll, they make a very nutritious snack, but you can also make them in different shapes and enjoy them as little antipasti with drinks or in place of potato chips.

Makes approx. 8 squares
250g (9oz) chickpea flour
10g (¼oz) salt
approx. 650ml (22fl oz) water
2 tsp finely chopped flat-leaf parsley
abundant vegetable oil, for greasing
  and frying

To serve
lemon wedges
crusty bread rolls

Combine the chickpea flour and salt in a saucepan. Gradually whisk in the water, making sure you get rid of all the lumps. Place the saucepan over a medium heat and keep whisking until you obtain a smooth and thick consistency – when ready, after about 3 minutes, the mixture will pull away from the sides of the pan.

Remove from the heat, stir in the chopped parsley and then pour the mixture over a lightly oiled flat tray or baking tray, spreading it evenly with the help of a spatula, or cover it with clingfilm, pressing down well over the mixture so it spreads evenly. Leave to cool completely.

When cool, cut the mixture into about eight squares. Heat plenty of vegetable oil in a deep frying pan over a high heat. When hot, deep-fry the *Panelle* for about 2–3 minutes until golden. Remove and drain on kitchen paper to absorb the excess oil.

These are delicious served immediately with a squeeze of lemon juice in crusty rolls.

MACCO DI FAVE

Split broad bean soup

This dish was around in Roman times when broad beans, cultivated in Greece, were introduced to Italy, and this nutritious pulse became popular all over rural Italy. This soup in particular, made with the dried variety, produces a lovely dense consistency, creating a perfect winter warmer. Made with just a few ingredients and sometimes with the addition of pasta, it was often a popular dish for farm workers, giving them all the nutrients they needed to work long hours in the fields.

Serves 4

500g (1lb 2oz) dried split broad beans, soaked overnight according to packet instructions
3 tbsp extra virgin olive oil, plus extra for drizzling
1 onion, finely chopped
1 celery stick, finely chopped
1 carrot, finely chopped
600ml (1 pint) vegetable stock
rustic bread, to serve

Drain and rinse the soaked broad beans.

Heat the olive oil in a large saucepan, add the onion, celery and carrot and sweat over a medium heat for a couple of minutes until softened. Stir in the broad beans and stock. Bring to the boil, then reduce the heat and simmer gently, whilst partially covered, for about 45 minutes until the broad beans are cooked. The beans will have absorbed quite a bit of the stock and the consistency will be dense and quite mushy.

Remove from the heat, divide the soup between individual bowls, then drizzle with a little olive oil and serve with rustic bread.

ZUPPA DI LENTICCHIE

Lentil soup

This is such an easy recipe to prepare. Simply put all the ingredients into a pot and leave to simmer – nutritious one-pot cooking at its best. Try to get small brown or green lentils if you can. To make it go further or, if you have some left over, add a little more water and add some small pasta shapes with the rest of the ingredients.

Serves 2–4

150g (5½oz) dried brown or green lentils, rinsed before use
1 celery stick, including leaves, roughly chopped
1 carrot, cut into chunks
1 garlic clove, lightly crushed and left whole
1 rosemary sprig
2 tablespoons tomato sauce or tomato passata
1 tbsp extra virgin olive oil, plus extra for drizzling
1 x 28g (1oz) vegetable stock pot or cube
1 medium potato, cut into chunks
approx. 800ml (28fl oz) water
2 tsp grated Parmesan cheese

Place all the ingredients (except the grated Parmesan) into a saucepan, bring to the boil, then reduce the heat and cook gently, whilst partially covered, for about 25 minutes until the lentils and vegetables are cooked – check your lentil packet for cooking times.

Remove from the heat and discard the rosemary sprig and garlic before serving. Stir in the grated Parmesan and serve in bowls with a drizzle of olive oil.

CANNELLINI ALL'UCCELLETTO

Cannellini beans in tomato sauce

This traditional Tuscan dish is very simple and quick to prepare. The name *Uccelletto* (from bird) suggests various theories: this dish was served with game, or the same ingredients of garlic and sage were used in game dishes, or it's because the beans were used instead of meat. Whichever are its origins, it makes a lovely side or main course dish. It's Italy's healthier version of the UK's baked beans. In fact, it is also delicious served on toasted bread, but please make it rustic bread!

To save some time, you can use 2 x 400g (14oz) tins of cannellini beans instead of the dried, if you prefer (see method).

Serves 4

250g (9oz) dried cannellini beans, soaked in plenty of cold water overnight

2 tbsp extra virgin olive oil, plus an extra good drizzle

8 sage leaves

1 garlic clove, finely sliced

½ red chilli, finely chopped (optional)

250ml (9fl oz) tomato passata

4 slices of rustic bread

sea salt

Drain and rinse the soaked cannellini beans, then place in a saucepan with plenty of cold water, bring to the boil and cook until tender, about 40–50 minutes – check the cooking time on your bean packet. Drain, reserving about 100ml (3½fl oz) of the cooking water.

Heat the olive oil in a heavy-based saucepan, add four sage leaves and fry over a medium heat for a minute or so until crispy, then add the garlic and chilli and sweat for a minute. Add the tomato passata and the reserved bean cooking water (if you are using canned beans, add can juice plus 50ml/3½ tbsp water) and some salt to taste, then reduce the heat, partially cover with a lid and simmer for 20 minutes.

Add the cannellini beans and simmer for a further 5 minutes until heated through. If you are using canned beans, add their liquid as well.

Just before the end of the cooking time, toast the bread slices. Heat a good drizzle of olive oil in a small frying pan, add the remaining sage leaves and fry over a medium heat for a minute or so until crispy.

Divide the bean mixture between individual bowls, top with the crispy sage and a drizzle of the sage-infused olive oil and serve with the toasted rustic bread.

FAVE E CICORIA

Split broad bean mash with greens

This simple but highly nutritious dish originates from rural Puglia where two main ingredients – fava beans and wild chicory – are widely available. With just the addition of olive oil, garlic and bay leaves for flavour, this dish really symbolizes the best of the old *cucina povera* and makes a delicious complete meal. If you can get dandelion or puntarelle from your greengrocer, remember to remove the heart, which you can then use in a salad (see *Insalata di Cuore di Cicoria* recipe on page 129). Otherwise, you can pick your own wild dandelion leaves or use long-stemmed broccoli instead.

Serves 4–6
400g (14oz) dried split broad beans, soaked
  overnight in plenty of cold water
4 bay leaves
5 garlic cloves, lightly crushed and left whole
4 tbsp extra virgin olive oil, plus extra
  for drizzling
600g (1lb 5oz) dandelion or puntarelle
  (gross weight)
sea salt and freshly ground black pepper

Drain and rinse the soaked broad beans. Place them in a saucepan, cover with plenty of fresh cold water, add the bay leaves and three garlic cloves, then bring to the boil and cook, partially covered, over a medium heat for about 45 minutes, until the beans are cooked through and tender. Remove from the heat, discard the bay leaves and garlic, then blend the beans until smooth using a handheld stick blender. Season to taste with salt and pepper. Set aside.

Remove the leaves from the dandelion (and the heart if using puntarelle) and save the roots to make a salad (see recipe intro). Take the leaves and blanch them in a pan of boiling water for a couple of minutes until tender. Drain well.

Heat the olive oil in a large frying pan, add the remaining two garlic cloves and sweat for a minute. Add the greens and stir-fry over a medium-to-high heat for 2–3 minutes, then season with salt and pepper.

Heat through the blended beans mixture, remove the whole garlic gloves and then serve with the greens, drizzled with a little olive oil.

BREAD

TORTA SALATA PUGLIESE

Onion and olive pie

A *Torta Salata* is an Italian savoury pie and there are many types with various fillings. This rustic Puglian-style pie is made with lots of onions, olives and local Caciocavallo cheese. As this cheese is difficult to obtain outside of the region, I have used a mix of Scamorza and Parmesan. It is delicious eaten warm or cold, and excellent for packed lunches and picnics.

Serves 6

For the dough

500g (1lb 2oz) strong white bread flour, plus extra for dusting

1 x 7g (⅛oz) sachet of fast-action dried yeast

1 tsp sea salt

50ml (2fl oz) white wine

2 tbsp extra virgin olive oil, plus extra for greasing

approx. 200ml (7fl oz) lukewarm water

For the filling

3 tbsp extra virgin olive oil

750g (1lb 10oz) onions, finely sliced

4 anchovy fillets, canned and left whole

120g (4¼oz) pitted black olives

15g (½oz) capers

70g (2½oz) Scamorza cheese, finely chopped

30g (1oz) grated Parmesan cheese

sea salt and freshly ground black pepper

Combine the flour, yeast and salt in a large bowl, add the wine and olive oil, then stir in enough lukewarm water to make a dough. Knead on a lightly floured work surface for a couple of minutes, then place in an oiled bowl, cover with a damp cloth and leave to rest in a warm place for about 1 hour or until the dough has doubled in size.

Now make the filling. Heat the olive oil in a large frying pan over a medium heat, add the onions and stir in the anchovy fillets until they dissolve. Reduce the heat and cook for 20 minutes until the onions have softened – if they exude a lot of liquid, increase the heat to evaporate the liquid off. Stir in the olives and capers and continue to cook over a gentle heat for 10 minutes. Remove from the heat and allow to cool. Add a little salt, if necessary.

Preheat the oven to 200°C fan/220°C/gas mark 7. Lightly grease a 26cm (10½in.) loose-bottomed round cake tin with olive oil.

Split the dough into two pieces, making one slightly larger. Roll out each piece into a round shape on a lightly floured surface. Take the larger round of dough and line the base and sides of the prepared cake tin with it. Fill with the onion filling, then sprinkle with the cheeses and a little black pepper. Place the other round of dough over the top and carefully crimp around the edges.

Bake in the oven for 35 minutes or until risen and golden brown. Remove from the oven, leave to cool slightly, then remove from the tin, slice and serve.

PASSATELLI IN BRODO

Breadcrumb and parmesan pasta

Originating in Emilia Romagna, this type of pasta consists of leftover stale bread, which is made into breadcrumbs enriched with egg and grated Parmesan. A couple of pinches of grated nutmeg and some lemon zest are also added for flavour. A simple tool, locally known as *fer,* is used to make the passatelli; it's a round perforated stainless steel press, attached to wooden handles. However, a potato ricer is just as good and does the job. This 'poor man's pasta' is traditionally served in a chicken stock, but it can also be cooked in a beef or vegetable stock or cooked and served as it is with a sauce.

Serves 4
100g (3½oz) stale breadcrumbs
100g (3½oz) grated Parmesan cheese, plus
  extra to serve
2 eggs
2 pinches of grated nutmeg
zest of ½ lemon
plain flour, for dusting
1 litre (1¾ pints) chicken stock
sea salt and freshly ground black pepper

Combine all the ingredients (except the flour for dusting and the chicken stock), including a little salt, in a bowl and mix well until you obtain a dough-like consistency. Form into a ball, wrap in clingfilm and leave to rest at room temperature for at least 1 hour.

Remove the clingfilm, then take about a quarter of the dough and press it through a potato ricer with large holes, cutting it off with a small sharp knife when it is about 5–6cm (2–2½in.) in length. You may get varying lengths and that's fine. Place them on a lightly floured board, taking care not to break them. Repeat with the rest of the dough, a quarter at a time.

In the meantime, bring the chicken stock to the boil in a large saucepan, then drop in all the passatelli and cook until they rise up to the surface. Remove from the heat and divide the mixture between four individual bowls. Serve with a little black pepper and a sprinkling of grated Parmesan.

MOZZARELLA IN CARROZZA

Mozzarella toastie

You can't beat a toastie and this traditional recipe from the region around Naples was first made as early as the 1800s as a way of using up stale bread and leftover cheese. One theory as to why this recipe is called *Carrozza* is that originally it was made using round slices of bread, resembling the wheels of a carriage. It's now a popular street food in Naples and the surrounding area, but it is enjoyed all over Italy, and Rome also claims to have its own version. Originally made with rustic bread, it is nowadays made with *Pane in Cassetta*, Italy's sliced white bread. However, you can make it with whatever leftover bread you have. Please ensure the mozzarella is well drained and dry before cooking.

Serve with a salad for a yummy lunch or snack; kids will also love this cheese toastie oozing with mozzarella. Serve one sandwich per person for a meal or half a sandwich as a snack.

Serves 2–4
2 eggs
abundant breadcrumbs, for coating
4 slices of bread
plain flour, for dusting
1 ball of mozzarella cheese (about
  125g/4½oz), drained and patted dry, then
  cut into slices
abundant vegetable oil, for deep-frying

Crack the eggs into a shallow bowl or dish and lightly beat. Place the breadcrumbs in another shallow dish or on a plate. Coat the bread slices in flour, shaking off the excess. Place the mozzarella slices on two slices of bread and sandwich together with the other two bread slices, pressing down firmly.

Carefully dip each sandwich in the beaten egg, making sure the edges are coated, too, then coat all over in the breadcrumbs. Place on a plate and leave to rest in the fridge for about 30 minutes. Dip each sandwich in the egg again and then coat in breadcrumbs as before.

Heat plenty of vegetable oil in a deep frying pan until hot, then deep-fry the sandwiches over a medium heat for about 3 minutes on each side, until golden. Turn over during frying so they have an even golden colour. Depending on the size of your pan, you may want to fry them one at a time. Drain on kitchen paper and serve.

PANE COTTO CON PATATE DI ADRIANA

Adriana's cooked bread and potatoes with rocket and pancetta

This old rural recipe from Puglia is a typical *cucina povera* dish made from using up stale bread and adding potatoes to make the dish go further. It's a hearty dish and you can add whatever other ingredients you have to hand, like tomatoes, local greens, onions, pancetta, etc, which is exactly what people did back then. Bacon is a perfectly good economical replacement to pancetta, if you prefer. This is my sister, Adriana's version, which she used to cook quite often when she lived in Puglia.

Serves 4

500g (1lb 2oz) potatoes
1.2 litres (2 pints) water
2 handfuls of rocket
200g (7oz) stale rustic bread, cut into
  thick chunks
4 tbsp extra virgin olive oil
120g (4½oz) pancetta or bacon,
  finely chopped
2 garlic cloves, lightly crushed and left whole
½ red chilli, finely sliced (optional)
sea salt

Peel the potatoes and cut into thick chunks, then place in a saucepan with the water and a little salt, bring to the boil and cook until nearly tender, about 10–15 minutes, until tender. Add the rocket and cook for a further 2 minutes or until the potatoes are cooked through.

Remove from the heat, add the bread chunks, cover with a lid to keep warm and leave to soak for about 5 minutes.

In the meantime, heat the olive oil in a frying pan, add the pancetta or bacon, garlic and chilli (if using) and sweat over a medium heat until the pancetta or bacon is cooked, about 5 minutes. Remove from the heat and then discard the garlic.

Combine the pancetta or bacon with the potato mixture, check for seasoning and, if necessary, add a little salt, then serve immediately.

CANDERLI AGLI SPINACI

Canderli with spinach

These bread dumplings originated in the mountainous Alpine region of Trentino Alto-Adige in northern Italy, making use of leftover bread and whatever else was to hand. Traditionally, speck, a cured meat of the region, is used, but in this version I have added spinach instead. You can enjoy the dumplings with the stock you cook them in or drained and tossed with melted butter and grated Parmesan. Either way, this makes a hearty, nutritious meal.

Serves 4 (makes approx. 14 balls)

150g (5½oz) bread
60ml (4 tbsp) milk
80g (3oz) butter
drizzle of extra virgin olive oil
½ onion, finely chopped
1 garlic clove, finely chopped
200g (7oz) cooked spinach (approx. 480g/1lb 1oz frozen spinach), drained and excess liquid squeezed out

2 eggs, lightly beaten
30g (1oz) grated Parmesan cheese, plus extra for sprinkling
30g (1oz) plain flour
pinch of grated nutmeg
approx. 1.5 litres (2¾ pints) vegetable stock (optional)
sea salt and freshly ground black pepper

Chop the bread into small pieces and combine with the milk in a bowl. Set aside.

Meanwhile, heat 20g (¾oz) of the butter with a drizzle of olive oil in a saucepan, add the onion and garlic and sweat over a medium heat for a couple of minutes, then stir in the squeezed-out cooked spinach and cook for a minute. Remove from the heat and leave to cool.

Combine the soaked bread with the spinach mixture, eggs, Parmesan, flour, nutmeg and a little salt and pepper to taste. Shape the mixture into about 14 walnut-sized balls.

Bring a large saucepan of either vegetable stock (if using) or salted water to the boil, then add the canderli, bring back to a simmer and cook for 15 minutes. Towards the end of the cooking time, melt the remaining butter in a small pan.

Gently lift the canderli out of the stock with a slotted spoon, place on a serving dish, pour over the melted butter, sprinkle with some grated Parmesan and serve immediately.

PAPPA AL POMODORO

Bread and tomato soup

This traditional Tuscan 'poor man's soup' is quite ancient in its origins, which became well known all over Italy after appearing in a newspaper article in the 1920s, and later the title of a popular Italian song. A simple thick soup of bread and tomatoes, it is the perfect way of using up stale bread. It is best made with fresh tomatoes, but you could make it with good-quality canned tomatoes instead. You can also enjoy it cold, so it's an ideal summer dish when tomatoes and basil are plentiful.

Serves 4
1kg (2lb 4oz) San Marzano-type tomatoes
3 tbsp extra virgin olive oil, plus extra
 for drizzling
3 garlic cloves – 2 crushed, 1 peeled and
 left whole
½ handful of basil leaves, plus a few stalks
 (chopped)
300g (10½oz) stale rustic bread
1 litre (1¾ pints) vegetable stock, heated

Cut a shallow cross in the bottom of each tomato and then blanch them in a pan or bowl of boiling water for a minute or so. Remove with a slotted spoon and when, cool enough to handle, remove the skin, cut the tomatoes into quarters and carefully remove the seeds. Do this into a fine sieve set over a bowl to catch the juices. Cut the tomato quarters into thin slices, then add the strained juice to the tomato slices.

Heat the olive oil in a saucepan, add the crushed garlic cloves and sweat for a minute with the basil stalks, then stir in the tomato slices and cook over a medium heat for about 10 minutes.

In the meantime, preheat the grill to high. Thickly slice the bread, place under the hot grill and lightly toast on both sides, then remove and rub on one side with the whole garlic clove.

Place the toasted bread in a large bowl, pour over some of the hot stock and leave for a few minutes until the bread crusts have softened. Once softened, place the softened bread in the pan with the tomatoes along with the rest of the hot stock, mixing well, then heat through, if necessary.

Serve immediately in individual bowls with a drizzle of olive oil and the basil leaves scattered over.

ACQUASALE

Fresella bread salad

This is similar to the Tuscan *Panzanella* salad, which uses stale bread. This recipe, originating from rural Puglia, uses *Fresella*, a double-baked bread, which can be found in Italian delis and is a really handy storecupboard ingredient, should you run out of bread. Obviously, *Fresella* was once made at home by placing slices of stale bread in a low oven and baking it until crispy – I still do this today when I have lots of bread. The *Fresella* keeps in an airtight container and is ideal to use in bread salads like this one, or in soups, or simply to enjoy as a snack with a drizzle of olive oil. To refresh the *Fresella*, simply sprinkle with a little water to soften it.

I have given you the traditional Puglian version of this recipe, using the summer vegetables that farmers grew or could be obtained easily. However you can, of course, enrich it with peppers, olives, capers, pickles, cooked beans and canned tuna.

Serves 4
1 small red onion, finely sliced
red wine vinegar, to taste
4 slices of Fresella
approx. 100ml (3½fl oz) water
200g (7oz) baby plum tomatoes, halved
1 celery stick, including leaves, finely sliced
½ cucumber, sliced
1 tsp dried oregano
40ml (1½fl oz) extra virgin olive oil, plus
  extra for drizzling
sea salt

Place the red onion in a small bowl and cover with red wine vinegar. Set aside for at least 30 minutes.

Meanwhile, place the *Fresella* slices on a plate and drizzle the water over them, then leave to soften, about 30 minutes. Once softened, break the *Fresella* up into chunks.

Drain the onion (keep the vinegar for another dish) and place in a bowl with the tomatoes, celery and cucumber. Sprinkle with the oregano and a little salt, then add the olive oil and mix well together. Add the *Fresella* chunks, mix well and then leave to rest at room temperature for about 1 hour before serving with a drizzle of olive oil.

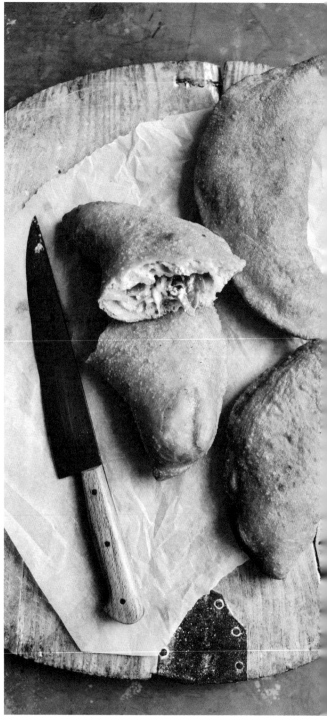

PIZZA FRITTA

Fried stuffed pizza

Pizza Fritta or fried pizza is a typical Neapolitan street food. Some are flat and, once the dough is fried, a simple topping of tomato sauce and cheese is added. Others are filled and then fried, like in this recipe. *Pizza Fritta* was born in Naples after WW2, when most of the ovens in the city had been destroyed in the bombings, so the Neapolitan pizza makers came up with the ingenious idea of frying the dough, which swells during cooking and is usually quicker to cook than baked pizza. It was such a success that this tradition lives on and you really can't visit Naples without enjoying a *Pizza Fritta* while wandering around the bustling chaos of the city.

Makes 4 large filled pizzas

For the dough
500g (1lb 2oz) strong white bread flour, plus extra for dusting
1 x 6g (⅛oz) dried yeast
12g (¼oz) sea salt
320ml (11fl oz) lukewarm water

For the filling
1 ball of mozzarella cheese (about 125g/4½oz), drained and finely chopped
6 x tbsp ricotta
80g (3oz) cooked ham, finely chopped
4 tbsp tomato sauce
4 basil leaves
20g (¾oz) grated Parmesan cheese
freshly ground black pepper

abundant vegetable oil, for frying

Combine the flour, yeast and salt in a large bowl, then gradually add the lukewarm water, mixing to make a dough. Tip out onto a lightly floured work surface and knead for 5 minutes. Cover and leave to rest for 10 minutes.

Cut the dough into four equal pieces, place on a lightly floured baking tray, cover with a damp cloth and leave to rise in a warm place for about 3½ hours or until doubled in size.

Take a piece of dough and roll it out on a lightly floured surface into a circle roughly 22cm (8½in.) in diameter. Place some mozzarella in the centre, then add some ricotta, ham, 1 tablespoon of the tomato sauce and a basil leaf. Sprinkle with some grated Parmesan and a little black pepper. Brush water around the edges, then fold over and seal the edges well. Repeat with the remaining pieces of dough and filling.

Heat plenty of vegetable oil in a large frying pan, then fry the calzones. Using a spoon, pour hot oil over the top – you will see each pizza swelling as it fries. Fry for 2–3 minutes until golden underneath, then flip over and continue to fry until golden all over. Remove from the pan and drain on kitchen paper, then serve.

GNOCCO FRITTO

Puffy fried bread rolls

Nothing to do with gnocchi, this traditional bread from Emilia Romagna is quite ancient in its origins and was first made during a time when nothing was wasted from the animal, so lard was used to enrich the dough. Over time, this once-rural bread substitute has become a popular street food and is also served in local restaurants as part of an antipasto, together with a selection of cured meats and cheese.

You will notice, as soon as the pieces of dough hit the hot oil, they become all lovely and puffy.

Makes approx. 40

For the starter
30g (1oz) strong white bread flour
4g (⅛oz) fast-action dried yeast
½ tsp white sugar
50ml (2fl oz) lukewarm water

For the dough
220g (8oz) strong white bread flour, plus extra
  for dusting
35g (1¼oz) lard, cut into small pieces
6g (⅛oz) sea salt
approx. 100ml (3½fl oz) lukewarm water

abundant vegetable oil, for greasing and frying

First make the starter. Combine all the ingredients in a small bowl, cover with a damp cloth and leave to rest in a warm place for 1 hour. You will see lots of bubbles appear on the surface.

Once you have a bubbly starter, make the dough. Place the flour in a bowl, stir in the starter, the pieces of lard and the salt and then gradually stir in enough lukewarm water to make a dough. Place on a lightly floured work surface and knead the dough for a couple of minutes, then place in an oiled bowl, cover with a damp cloth and leave to rest in a warm place for 1½–2 hours or until the dough has tripled in size.

Roll out the risen dough to a thickness of 3mm (⅛in.), cut into strips 5cm (2in.) wide and then cut out diamond shapes, about 8cm (3¼in.) in length.

Heat plenty of vegetable oil in a deep frying pan over a high heat until hot, then add a few of the diamond shapes at a time and fry for about 1 minute or so until golden and puffy. Remove with a slotted spoon and leave to drain on kitchen paper. Repeat until you have fried all the diamond shapes, making sure the oil is hot before you fry each batch.

These are best served immediately with a selection of cured meats, cheese and pickles.

POTATOES

TORTA SALATA DI SPINACI E PATATE

Spinach and potato pie

Torte Salate in Italy refers to savoury pies and these are a great way of using up leftovers, which are baked inside a pastry case. I have used a traditional pastry (using extra virgin olive oil and water) for this recipe, sometimes referred to as *Pasta Matta*. This simple pie of spinach, potatoes and cheese makes a substantial and complete meal. I like using frozen spinach, which normally comes packaged in cubes, as these are really handy for adding into dishes like this or for soups and stews. This pie can be served hot, warm or cold.

Serves 6

For the pastry
400g (14oz) plain flour or '00' pasta flour, sifted,
  plus extra for dusting
8g (¼oz) sea salt
30ml (1fl oz) olive oil
200ml (7fl oz) water

For the filling
800g (1lb 12oz) potatoes
1 rosemary sprig, needles stripped
drizzle of extra virgin olive oil, plus extra for greasing
1 garlic clove, lightly crushed and left whole
300g (10½oz) frozen spinach, defrosted
1 tbsp breadcrumbs (fresh, stale or dried)
30g (1oz) grated Parmesan cheese
120g (4¼oz) pancetta, cubed
150g (5½oz) provolone cheese, cut into small pieces
sea salt and freshly ground black pepper

Make the pastry by combining the flour and salt in a large bowl, then add the olive oil and gradually stir in the water to make a smooth dough. Wrap in clingfilm and leave to rest at room temperature while you make the filling.

Peel the potatoes and cut into small cubes. Cook the potato cubes in a large pan of boiling water until just tender, about 7 minutes – be careful not to overcook them as they will fall apart. Drain, leave to cool and then sprinkle the rosemary needles all over.

Heat a drizzle of olive in a frying pan, sweat the garlic over a medium heat for 1 minute, then stir in the spinach and cook for a minute or so. Season with salt and pepper. Remove from the heat, leave to cool and then squeeze out any excess liquid.

Preheat the oven to 160°C fan/180°C/gas mark 4. Lightly grease a 28cm (11in.) round pie dish or tart tin.

Roll out the pastry on a lightly floured work surface to a thickness of about 5mm (¼in.) and line the base and sides of the prepared dish or tin with the pastry. Discard the garlic clove. Arrange the spinach over the bottom of the pastry case in an even layer, then sprinkle with the breadcrumbs, half the grated Parmesan, the pancetta cubes, the provolone pieces and the rosemary potato cubes and finish off with the remaining grated Parmesan.

Bake in the oven for about 25 minutes until golden brown. Remove from the oven and rest for 5 minutes before serving.

GATTO' DI PATATE NAPOLETANO

Neapolitan mashed potato cake

This traditional Neapolitan recipe dates back to the 1760s, when it was apparently made for a royal wedding and French chefs were called in to prepare the banquet. It was named 'gateau of potatoes' as it resembles a cake, which over time the Neapolitans referred to as *Gatto*. Although it has noble roots, this recipe is perfect for using up leftovers of ham, cheese, salami and any other cured meats you have in your fridge. Simple and economical to make, it is very nutritious and can be eaten hot or cold as a meal by itself, with perhaps a green salad to accompany.

Serves 4

40g (1½oz) butter, plus extra for greasing

30g (1oz) dried breadcrumbs

700g (1lb 9oz) potatoes, peeled and cut
  into chunks

2 eggs

30g (1oz) grated Parmesan cheese

50ml (2fl oz) hot milk

100g (3½oz) Scamorza cheese, cut into
  small cubes

20g (¾oz) Asiago cheese, cut into
  small cubes

1 ball of mozzarella cheese (about
  125g/4½oz), drained and
  roughly chopped

80g (3oz) cooked ham, cut into small pieces

sea salt and freshly ground black pepper

Preheat the oven to 180°C fan/200°C/gas mark 6. Grease a 20cm (8in.) round sandwich cake tin with a little of the butter and then coat with some of the breadcrumbs, tapping out the excess.

Cook the potatoes in a large pan of boiling water for about 20 minutes or until tender, then drain well and mash. Mix in some salt and pepper, the eggs, grated Parmesan, 30g (1oz) of the butter, the hot milk, half the Scamorza, Asiago and mozzarella cheeses and half the ham.

Spoon half the mashed potato mixture evenly into the prepared cake tin, scatter the rest of the ham and cheeses over and then top with the remaining mash in an even layer. Dot with the remaining butter and sprinkle with the remaining breadcrumbs.

Bake in the oven for about 40 minutes until risen and golden all over. Remove from the oven, leave to rest for 5 minutes and then serve.

PATATE 'MPACCHIUSE CALABRESI

Calabrian-style sauté potatoes

Believe it or not, the southern Italian region of Calabria is famous for its potatoes, sweet red Tropea onions and even mushrooms, which grow in the Sila forest. So, it makes sense to put these three ingredients together, not forgetting another of Calabria's specialities, pungent red chillies. The word '*mpacchiuse* in the regional dialect means 'to stick' as this is what the potatoes tend to do in the frying pan. The potatoes should be a little crispy on the outside but soft and fluffy inside. I love chilli, but you can, of course, leave it out or use less.

Serves 2–4
600g (1lb 5oz) potatoes
3 tbsp extra virgin olive oil
1 garlic clove, lightly crushed and left whole
1 red chilli, finely chopped (optional)
1 red onion, finely sliced
100g (3½oz) chestnut mushrooms, cleaned and sliced
sea salt

Peel the potatoes and cut them into 5mm (¼in.) slices.

Heat the olive oil in a non-stick frying pan, add the garlic and sweat over a medium heat for a couple of minutes, taking care not to let it burn. Discard the garlic, then add the potato slices to the pan, along with a little salt and the chilli (if using). Cover with a lid and cook over a medium-low heat for about 6 minutes.

Carefully turn the potato slices over, add the onion and mushrooms on top, cover with a lid and continue to cook for about 15 minutes, until everything is cooked and the potatoes are golden.

Remove from the heat and serve.

PATATE IN UMIDO AL POMODORO

Potatoes in tomato sauce

This simple dish can be served as a side dish or is equally delicious on its own with some rustic bread to mop up the tomato sauce.

Serves 4–6

4 tbsp extra virgin olive oil
2 garlic cloves, finely chopped
1 celery stick, finely chopped
1 x 400g (14oz) can chopped tomatoes or
  400g (14oz) tomato passata
1kg (2lb 4oz) potatoes, peeled and cut into
  equal, medium-sized chunks
approx. 300ml (10fl oz) water
handful of flat-leaf parsley, finely chopped
sea salt

Heat the olive oil in a large saucepan, add the garlic and celery and sweat over a medium heat for a couple of minutes. Stir in the tomatoes and a little salt and cook for 10 minutes. Add the potatoes and just enough water to cover them, bring to the boil, then reduce the heat, partially cover with a lid and simmer for 30 minutes until the potatoes are cooked.

If there is too much liquid left in the pan, increase the heat for the last 5 minutes of the cooking time, remove the lid and cook until most of the liquid has evaporated.

Remove from the heat, then stir in the parsley, taking care not to break up the potatoes, and serve.

PATATE ARRAGANATE

Potatoes in oregano

This traditional dish, originating from the southern region of Basilicata, takes its name *Arraganate* from meaning 'with oregano'. It's a simple bake of potatoes, oregano, fresh breadcrumbs and tomatoes. It can also be enriched with other ingredients and cheese, but I like this simple version that can be served as a side dish to accompany meat but is also delicious as a meal in itself, perhaps served with a green salad.

Serves 2–4

40g (1½oz) crustless rustic bread
1 garlic clove, finely diced
handful of flat-leaf parsley, finely chopped
1 tsp dried oregano
¼ red chilli, finely chopped (optional)
approx. 3 tbsp extra virgin olive oil
500g (1lb 2oz) potatoes, unpeeled, finely
   sliced into rounds
8 baby plum tomatoes, cut into quarters
2 tbsp water
sea salt

Preheat the oven to 180°C fan/200°C/gas mark 6.

Take the soft bread and, with your hands, crumble it into breadcrumbs, then combine with the garlic, parsley, oregano and chilli (if using). Set aside.

Drizzle the base of an ovenproof dish (I used a 20 x 20cm/8 x 8in. one) with 1 tablespoon of the olive oil. Place a layer of potato slices on top, then sprinkle with a little salt, some of the breadcrumb mixture, some tomato quarters and a drizzle of olive oil. Make another layer like this one, then if you have ingredients left over, continue making layers like these until you have used everything, ending with the breadcrumb mixture and a drizzle of olive oil. I made two layers in my ovenproof dish. Pour the water around the sides of the dish.

Cover with foil and bake in the oven for 45 minutes. Remove the foil and continue to bake for a further 10 minutes until cooked through and golden. Remove from the oven and rest for 5 minutes before serving.

TIELLA DI PATATE, RISO E CARCIOFI

Potato, rice and artichoke bake

This typical dish from Bari is traditionally made with mussels, but this is a vegetarian version made with artichokes. It originates from the region's *cucina povera*, adding rice and potatoes to bulk up the dish that was a popular meal in rural communities. Over time, this once-impoverished dish could be found in good restaurants in the Puglia region. *Tiella* is the name given to the terracotta dish that was used to cook this recipe, but, of course, any ovenproof dish can be used. It is normally prepared with fresh artichokes, but these are often not easily obtainable, so I have used preserved ones, which you can keep in your store cupboard and spare you the task of cleaning them!

Serves 4

1kg (2lb 4oz) potatoes, peeled and cut into 5mm (¼in.) thick slices
225g (8oz) arborio rice
200g (7oz) whole baby plum tomatoes
1 red onion, finely sliced
extra virgin olive oil, for drizzling
juice of 1 lemon
2 garlic cloves, diced

handful of flat-leaf parsley leaves, finely chopped
100g (3½oz) grated pecorino cheese
1 x 250g (9oz) jar of chargrilled preserved artichokes
450ml (16fl oz) vegetable stock
sea salt

Place the potato slices in a bowl of cold water and leave for about 20 minutes while you prepare the other ingredients. Rinse the rice under plenty of cold running water and drain well.

Combine the tomatoes and onion in a bowl, sprinkle with a little salt, squeeze of lemon juice and a drizzle of olive oil. Set aside.

Preheat the oven to 160°C fan/180°C/gas mark 4. Combine the garlic, parsley and pecorino in a separate bowl. Drain the potatoes and dry well in a clean tea towel, then place in a bowl, drizzle with olive oil and toss to coat.

Drizzle a little olive oil in an ovenproof dish. Place a layer of potato slices in the dish, scatter half the mixed tomatoes and onion over the top, then add half the rice, followed by three artichokes. Sprinkle over half the pecorino mix. Repeat these layers, finishing with the remaining pecorino mix.

Pour the vegetable stock around the sides of the dish, then cover with foil and bake in the oven for 1 hour 10 minutes. Remove the foil and continue to bake for 20 minutes until crispy on top. Remove from the oven and serve.

EGGS

UOVA ALLA MONACHINA

Stuffed fried eggs

This is a dish that the Neapolitans adopted a long time ago from French cuisine. It actually has noble origins and was made for the wedding of King Ferdinando IV and Maria Carolina of Austria – apparently she was not keen on Neapolitan flavours, so French chefs were sent to the rescue and this dish was served as part of the canapés for the wedding feast. However, this recipe also became a popular dish for everyone who enjoyed the nutritious stuffed eggs as a main course. Nowadays, this recipe is often cooked during Easter to enjoy as a starter or with drinks. These really are tasty but very filling!

Serves 6

6 eggs

25g (1oz) butter

25g (1oz) plain flour, plus extra for dusting

125ml (4fl oz) milk

25g (1oz) grated Parmesan cheese

2 tsp chopped chives (optional)

2 eggs, beaten with a little sea salt

breadcrumbs, dried, for coating

abundant vegetable oil, for frying

sea salt and freshly ground black pepper

Cook the 6 whole eggs in a pan of boiling water for about 8–10 minutes until they are hard-boiled. Remove from the heat, drain and then place in cold water and leave to cool.

In the meantime, make the béchamel sauce. Melt the butter in a small saucepan, take it off the heat and quickly whisk in the flour, then gradually whisk in the milk. Return to the heat and cook over a low heat, whisking, until the sauce begins to thicken. The consistency will be thicker than a white sauce you would make for a lasagne, for example. Remove from the heat, stir in the grated Parmesan, a little salt and pepper and the chives. Set aside.

Remove the shells from the eggs and cut the eggs in half lengthways. Carefully remove the egg yolks and place in a fine sieve over the béchamel sauce in the pan, then press into the sauce using the back of a teaspoon. Mix the sieved egg yolk and béchamel sauce together until combined. Fill the egg cavities with the béchamel mixture and gently press both egg halves together. Dust the filled eggs in a little flour, dip in the beaten egg and then coat in breadcrumbs.

Heat plenty of vegetable oil in a deep saucepan until hot (or use a deep fat fryer), then deep-fry the eggs for about a minute until golden all over. Remove with a slotted spoon and leave to drain on kitchen paper. Leave to rest for a couple of minutes, then slice the eggs or leave them whole to serve.

TORTA DI FRITTATA AL FORNO CON ZUCCHINE E SCAMORZA

Baked frittata cake with courgettes and scamorza

A frittata or omelette is a great way of using up leftovers like vegetables, cheese, cured meats, etc, and it makes a quick, simple and economical nutritious meal. This frittata is baked and has slices of cheese sandwiched in the middle, a bit like a cake, so when you slice into it, you get a lovely gooey cheesy centre. I have used Scamorza, which is a hard smoked mozzarella, but you can use any cheese you have to hand. Serve with a tomato salad for a delicious meal.

Serves 4

3 tbsp extra virgin olive oil
2 large courgettes (approx. 600g/1lb 5oz total
  weight), finely sliced
1 red onion, finely chopped
6 eggs
6 basil leaves, roughly torn
20g (¾oz) grated Parmesan cheese
20g (¾oz) fresh, dried or stale breadcrumbs
  (optional)
200g (7oz) Scamorza cheese, thinly sliced
sea salt and freshly ground black pepper

Preheat the oven to 180°C fan/200°C/gas mark 6. Line a round ovenproof dish (approx. 20cm/8in. diameter) with baking paper.

Heat the olive oil in a large frying pan, add the courgettes and stir-fry over a medium heat for 3 minutes. Add the onion and continue to cook for about 5 minutes until the vegetables have softened. Remove from the heat and leave to cool.

Beat the eggs in a bowl, add the basil, Parmesan, breadcrumbs (if using) and a little salt and pepper to taste. Combine the egg mixture with the vegetables. Pour half the egg mixture into the prepared ovenproof dish, place the slices of Scamorza cheese on top, then pour over the remaining egg mixture.

Bake in the oven for 20 minutes until firm and golden. Remove from the oven, slice and serve.

PALLOTTE CACIO E OVA

Cheese and egg balls

This traditional dish from the Abruzzo region was originally served as a main meal in place of expensive meat, hence placing the balls in tomato sauce as you would do with meatballs. But it's also a great way of using up leftover bread and cheese. You can use whatever hard cheese you have lying around that can easily be grated, like I did in this recipe. You can serve the balls in tomato sauce or they are equally delicious as they are – in fact, smaller ones would be ideal to serve with drinks.

Makes 10 balls

For the tomato sauce
2 tbsp extra virgin olive oil
½ onion, finely chopped
400ml (14fl oz) tomato passata
sea salt and freshly ground black pepper

For the cheese and egg balls
100g (3½oz) stale bread, crusts removed
150g (5½oz) mixed grated cheeses (85g/3oz Parmesan, 30g/1oz Cheddar, 35g/1¼oz Jarlsberg)
3 eggs
1 small garlic clove, diced
1 tbsp finely chopped flat-leaf parsley

abundant vegetable or sunflower oil, for frying

First make the tomato sauce. Heat the olive oil in a saucepan, add the onion and sweat over a medium heat for a couple of minutes until softened. Stir in the tomato passata and some salt and leave to bubble away over a low-medium heat for about 15 minutes.

In the meantime, make the cheese and egg balls. Grate the stale bread into breadcrumbs and then combine with the mixed cheeses, the eggs, garlic, parsley and some salt and pepper, until the ingredients all stick together. Take a small amount of this mixture in the palm of your hand and roll it around to make a ball, about the size of a walnut. Repeat to make 10 balls in total.

Heat the oil in a deep pan over a high heat until hot, then drop in the *Pallotte*, a few at a time, and fry for 2–3 minutes until golden on all sides, turning once during cooking. Remove with a slotted spoon and drain on kitchen paper. When all the *Pallotte* are fried, transfer them into the tomato sauce and cook over a low heat for about 10 minutes, then serve.

BRACIOLE DI UOVA IN POMODORO

Mini filled omelettes in tomato sauce

In Neapolitan, *Braciole* normally refers to thin slices of beef or pork, which are filled, rolled up and cooked in tomato sauce. In this recipe, eggs are used to substitute the meat and would often be made when meat was too expensive or forbidden to consume for religious reasons. It's often a popular dish for children in Italy, and served with a green salad or steamed greens and plenty of good bread, it makes a delicious main meal. Serve 1 or 2 omelettes per person.

Serves 2–4

For the sauce
1 tbsp extra virgin olive oil
¼ onion, finely chopped
1 x 400g (14oz) can chopped tomatoes
½ handful of basil leaves
sea salt and freshly ground black pepper

For the omelettes
4 eggs
20g (¾oz) grated Parmesan cheese
drizzle of extra virgin olive oil
1 small garlic clove, finely diced
½ handful of flat-leaf parsley leaves,
* finely chopped*

First make the sauce. Heat the olive oil in a saucepan, add the onion and sweat over a medium heat for a couple of minutes until softened. Stir in the tomatoes, then rinse the can with a little water and add this (about a quarter of a can) to the pan. Add a little salt and the basil leaves. Reduce the heat and simmer gently, partially covered, for about 25 minutes.

Meanwhile, prepare the omelettes. Combine the eggs, a little salt and pepper and 10g (¼oz) of the grated Parmesan in a jug. Heat a drizzle of olive oil in a small, non-stick frying pan (about 15cm/6in. diameter) over a medium heat, then add a quarter of the egg mixture and make a small omelette. Tilt the pan so the eggs cover the surface of the pan, cook briefly, then tilt the pan again to let any runny egg run to the sides; cook until just set. Remove from the pan and place on kitchen paper. Repeat until you have four small omelettes.

On each omelette, sprinkle the remaining Parmesan, garlic and parsley. Carefully roll up each omelette, then secure with a cocktail stick and place in a larger frying pan so they all fit nicely together.

Blend the tomato sauce until smooth using a handheld stick blender, then pour over the omelettes in the pan, cover with a lid and heat through gently. Remove from the heat and serve immediately.

CRESPELLE AL PROSCIUTTO E FORMAGGIO

Filled savoury pancakes

These savoury pancakes are simple, nourishing and always a favourite, especially with kids. You can fill them with any other cheese or cured meats you have to hand. You can also make and assemble the pancakes in advance and simply bake them just before serving with a crunchy mixed salad for a delicious meal.

Makes 8 pancakes, serves 4
250g (9oz) plain flour, sifted
pinch of sea salt
4 eggs
500ml (18fl oz) milk
40g (1½ oz) butter, melted, plus extra for greasing
  and dotting
8 tbsp ricotta
300g (10½oz) cooked ham, roughly chopped
2 balls of mozzarella cheese (each about
  125g/4½oz), well drained and roughly chopped
30g (1oz) grated Parmesan cheese

Place the flour and salt in a bowl, whisk in the eggs and then gradually whisk in the milk, ensuring no lumps remain, until you have a smooth batter. Stir in the melted butter.

Place a non-stick frying pan (about 20cm/8in. diameter) over a medium-to-high heat, grease it with a little butter, then add a ladleful of batter in the centre of the pan. Swirl the pan around so that the mixture runs to all the sides and fry for a minute or so until the bottom is golden, then flip over to the other side and cook for a further minute until golden. Transfer to a plate and set aside. Repeat until you have used up all the batter.

Meanwhile, preheat the oven to 180°C fan/200°C/gas mark 6. Lightly grease an ovenproof dish with a little butter.

Spread a tablespoon of ricotta over each pancake, then place some of the ham and mozzarella onto each pancake. Roll up each pancake, taking care the filling does not escape. Put the filled pancakes into the greased dish, slightly overlapping each other. Dot with butter and sprinkle with the grated Parmesan.

Bake in the oven for 10–15 minutes until the mozzarella has melted nicely. Remove from the oven and serve immediately.

GNOCCHI ALLA GRATIROUELA

Egg and Parmesan gnocchi

This soft pillowy variety of gnocchi originates from Lombardy in northern Italy. Simply made with flour, water, cheese and eggs, they are a delight. They are so soft, you have to be careful when handling them once cooked, so avoid mixing them with a spoon.

Serves 4

For the gnocchi
500ml (18fl oz) water
30g (1oz) butter
pinch of sea salt
250g (9oz) '00' pasta flour
160g (5¾oz) grated Parmesan cheese,
  plus extra for serving
6 egg yolks

For the tomato sauce
2 tbsp extra virgin olive oil
½ onion, finely chopped
1 x 400g (14oz) can chopped tomatoes
a few basil leaves, roughly torn
sea salt

First make the gnocchi. Place the water, butter and salt in a medium saucepan, bring to the boil, then gradually mix in the flour. Reduce the heat and keep beating until the mixture comes away from the sides of the pan. Remove from the heat and leave to cool.

Once cool, add a little of the grated Parmesan and one egg yolk and mix well. Continue until you have added all the Parmesan and egg yolks, mixing well between each addition. Tip the mixture onto a work surface and gently knead into a smooth dough. Leave to rest for 30 minutes, (no need to cover.)

In the meantime, make the tomato sauce. Heat the olive oil in a saucepan and sweat the onion over a medium heat until softened. Add the tomatoes, rinsing the can with some water (about half a can) and adding along with the basil leaves and a little salt to taste.

continues overleaf

Cut the gnocchi dough into quarters, then take each piece and roll out into a long, thin sausage and cut across into small gnocchi, each about 2.5–3cm (1–1¼in.) in length. Using a grater or zester, press the gnocchi lightly against it to get the classic indentations, or do this using the tines of a fork.

Bring a large pot of salted water to the boil, then drop in the gnocchi and cook until they rise. Carefully scoop out the cooked gnocchi with a slotted spoon onto a large plate or bowl. Add some tomato sauce, then more gnocchi on top, and repeat this until all the ingredients are used; ending with the remaining tomato sauce on top. Serve immediately with a sprinkling of grated Parmesan.

PASTA

TESTAROLI

Lunigiana pasta

This ancient pasta dish from the Lunigiana region of northern Tuscany, simply made with flour and water, is traditionally cooked on a hot flat terracotta or cast-iron surface locally known as a *testo*. But you can obtain the same result with a heavy-based frying pan. Once the thick pancake-like batter is cooked on both sides, you cut it into the traditional diamond shapes and cook in a pan of salted, boiling water as you would with gnocchi. In the local *trattorie*, this pasta is dressed with a basil pesto sauce.

Serves 4

For the pesto sauce
3 handfuls of basil leaves
50g (1¾oz) grated Parmesan cheese
approx. 50ml (1fl oz) extra virgin olive oil

For the pasta dough
300g (10½oz) '00' pasta flour
pinch of sea salt
450ml (16fl oz) water

olive oil, for brushing

To make the pesto, place all the ingredients in a small blender and whizz together until you obtain a smooth paste. You may need to add a little more olive oil, but not too much. Set aside.

Place the flour and salt in a bowl, then gradually whisk in the water to make a thick, smooth batter.

Heat a small (approx. 20cm/8in. in diameter) heavy-based frying pan over a high heat, lightly brush a little olive oil over it and then add a ladleful of the batter. Cook for about 3 minutes on one side, then flip over and continue to cook for a minute on the other side. Transfer to a plate and set aside. Brush the pan with a little more olive oil and continue making as above.

Cut the circles of cooked batter into 4cm (1½in.) strips, then cut into diamond shapes, 8cm (3¼in.) in length – some will be smaller and it doesn't really matter if you don't make them into perfect diamonds.

Bring a large saucepan of salted water to the boil, then drop in a few *testaroli* at a time and cook for a couple of minutes until they rise to the top. Transfer to a heatproof bowl using a slotted spoon and keep warm while you cook the remaining *testaroli*.

Place the basil pesto sauce in a large serving bowl, add the *testaroli* and, with the help of a little hot pasta water, mix together well and then serve immediately.

PASTA ALLO SCARPARIELLO

Neapolitan pasta with tomato and cheese

It is said that this traditional Neapolitan pasta dish originated in the shoemakers' district (hence its name in dialect) when the leftover tomato sauce from Sunday's ragù was added, plus pieces of cheese to enrich the dish. As the recipe evolved, fresh tomatoes were used instead and a combination of grated pecorino and Parmesan was added at the end to give the dish a nice creamy finish. You could say it's almost like *Cacio e Pepe* with tomato and chilli. Simple, delicious and nutritious with very few ingredients needed, I'm sure it will become a favourite.

Paccheri is a typical Neapolitan pasta, shaped like large hollow tubes, however, if you prefer, you can use spaghetti or linguine.

Serves 4
320g (11½oz) dried paccheri pasta
5 tbsp extra virgin olive oil
2 garlic cloves, lightly crushed and left whole
½ red chilli, finely chopped
500g (1lb 2oz) baby plum tomatoes, cut in half
8 basil leaves, plus extra for garnish
50g (1¾oz) grated pecorino cheese
50g (1¾oz) grated Parmesan cheese
sea salt

Place a large pot of salted water over the heat, bring to the boil and then cook the paccheri according to the packet instructions until al dente.

Meanwhile, heat the olive oil in a large frying pan, add the garlic and chilli and sweat over a medium heat for a minute. Stir in the tomatoes, basil and a little salt and cook over a medium heat for about 7 minutes until the tomatoes have softened.

Drain the pasta, keeping a little of the cooking water. Add the pasta to the tomatoes, then add the pecorino and Parmesan and the reserved hot cooking water (a couple of tablespoons) and stir well over a medium heat for a minute or so until all well amalgamated.

Remove from the heat and serve immediately.

LINGUINE ALLA PUTTANESCA

Linguine with tomatoes, capers and black olives

This typical Neapolitan dish is sometimes referred to as *Pasta alla Marinara* or simply as *Con Olive e Capperi*, which are common ingredients in this part of Italy. The name *Puttanesca* came about in the mid twentieth century when it was claimed that this dish was served in the brothels of Naples – *puttana* means 'whore' in Italian. Another theory was that a restaurant owner on the island of Ischia put together this dish when a group of late-night customers asked him to make *Una Puttanata Qualsiasi* – in other words, make whatever you've got to hand. And that is exactly what he did with the ingredients he found in his kitchen. Whatever the reason behind its title, this spicy pasta dish is quick and simple to prepare with storecupboard ingredients.

Serves 4
4 tbsp extra virgin olive oil
4 garlic cloves, lightly crushed and left whole
4 anchovy fillets
½ red chilli, finely chopped
40g (1½oz) capers
2 x 400g (14oz) cans chopped tomatoes
couple of pinches of dried oregano
80g (3oz) pitted black olives
320g (11½oz) dried linguine
handful of flat-leaf parsley, finely chopped
sea salt

Heat the olive oil in a large frying pan, add the garlic, anchovy fillets, chilli and capers and sweat over a medium heat until the anchovies have dissolved, about 2 minutes. Stir in the tomatoes, oregano and a little salt to taste. Cover with a lid and cook over a medium-low heat for 15 minutes. Stir in the olives and continue to cook for a further 10 minutes.

In the meantime, bring a large pot of salted water to the boil, add the linguine and cook according to the packet instructions until al dente.

Drain the linguine, reserving a little of the pasta cooking water, then add both to the tomato sauce. Cook over a high heat for a minute, mixing well. Remove from the heat, discard the garlic, then stir in the parsley and serve immediately.

PASTA E PATATE

Pasta with potatoes

This reminds me of my childhood when we would often have this carb-laden comfort dish, especially during winter. So simple to prepare in one pot, I am sure you will love it and it will become a firm favourite. For vegetarians, omit the pancetta and make sure the cheeses you use are suitable for vegetarians. I like the subtle smoky flavour of Scamorza, but if you can't find it, simply use another cheese you have or add more Parmesan. Adding the Parmesan rind is a great way of using all parts of the cheese as well as adding extra flavour. A mixture of pasta shapes is also a good way of using up leftover dried pasta in packets, but if you prefer, simply use one shape.

Serves 4

5 tbsp extra virgin olive oil
60g (2¼oz) pancetta, finely chopped
1 onion, finely chopped
1 small carrot, finely chopped
handful of celery leaves, roughly chopped
8 baby plum tomatoes, sliced in half
900g (2lb) potatoes, peeled and cut into small cubes
30g (1oz) Parmesan rind, finely chopped
approx. 1litre (34fl oz) hot water
300g (10½oz) tubetti or macaroni, broken-up
  spaghetti or broken-up tagliatelle, or a mixture
160g (5¾oz) Scamorza cheese, cut into small cubes
sea salt and freshly ground black pepper
grated Parmesan cheese, to serve (optional)

Heat the olive oil in a large saucepan over a medium heat, add the pancetta and stir-fry for a couple of minutes until it begins to colour. Add the onion, carrot, celery leaves and tomatoes and sweat over a medium heat for 2–3 minutes. Stir in the potatoes, Parmesan rind and some salt and then add enough hot water to cover. Cover with a lid and cook over a medium heat for 40 minutes.

Add the pasta and more hot water to cover, (you may need more or less liquid, so add this gradually as you would with risotto) and continue to cook over a medium heat for 10–15 minutes until the pasta is cooked and most of the liquid has been absorbed.

Remove from the heat, stir in the cheese, then leave to rest for a couple of minutes before serving. Serve with a grating of black pepper and a sprinkling of grated Parmesan.

SPAGHETTI AMMUDDICATI
Spaghetti with anchovies and breadcrumbs

This simple pasta dish really is a symbol of the *cucina povera* when people made use of leftover bread and added it to pasta dishes like this one. A popular combination was with anchovies, which were easily obtainable and economical throughout southern Italy. It may seem like a really impoverished dish, but with good breadcrumbs, anchovies and extra virgin olive oil, the flavours really enhance the pasta and I'm sure it will become a favourite recipe, making good use of storecupboard ingredients. If you can, make your own breadcrumbs from good rustic bread, as it really will make all the difference.

Serves 4
320g (11½oz) dried spaghetti
4 tbsp extra virgin olive oil, plus extra for drizzling
40g (1½oz) good-quality breadcrumbs, preferably
* homemade (fresh or stale)*
2 garlic cloves, lightly crushed and left whole
4 anchovy fillets
handful of flat-leaf parsley, finely chopped
1 tsp dried chilli flakes
sea salt
squeeze of lemon juice, to serve

Place a large pot of salted water over the heat, bring to the boil and then cook the spaghetti according to the packet instructions until al dente. Drain well, reserving a little of the cooking water.

In the meantime, heat a drizzle of olive oil in a small, non-stick frying pan over a medium-to-high heat, then add the breadcrumbs and toast lightly until golden for about a minute; taking care not to burn. Remove from the heat, place the breadcrumbs onto a plate and set aside.

In a larger frying pan, heat the olive oil over a medium heat, add the garlic and anchovy fillets and cook until the anchovies have dissolved. Increase the heat, add the drained cooked spaghetti with the reserved hot cooking water, then cook for a minute or so, stirring well.

Remove from the heat, stir in the parsley, chilli flakes and the toasted breadcrumbs, then serve immediately with a squeeze of lemon.

ORECCHIETTE CON BROCCOLI

Orecchiette pasta with broccoli

This classic pasta dish from Puglia is normally made with *cime di rape* (rape tops), which are quite difficult to find unless you're in Italy. Broccoli is a great substitute; economical, easy to find and packed with vitamins and other nutrients. This is such a simple dish to make using very few ingredients. The anchovies add a lovely saltiness, but you can omit them, if you prefer. If you can't find *orecchiette* pasta, then simply use spaghetti.

Serves 4
2 heads of broccoli, cut into florets (approx.
   650g/1lb 7oz total weight)
4 tbsp extra virgin olive oil
4 garlic cloves, finely chopped
½ red chilli, finely chopped
4 anchovy fillets
300g (10½oz) dried orecchiette pasta
sea salt

Cook the broccoli in a large pan of slightly salted boiling water for about 10 minutes until tender.

Meanwhile, heat the olive oil in a large frying pan, add the garlic, chilli and anchovy fillets and sweat over a medium heat until the anchovies have dissolved.

With the help of a spider strainer, pick up the cooked broccoli from its pan of water and transfer it into the frying pan, then stir-fry for a couple of minutes.

Bring the pan of broccoli water back to the boil, then add the *orecchiette* pasta and cook according to the packet instructions until al dente.

Add a couple of tablespoons of the hot pasta cooking water to the frying pan and continue to cook for a couple of minutes. Take a potato masher and gently mash the broccoli.

When the *orecchiette* is cooked, remove using a slotted spoon (or the spider strainer) and add to the broccoli, mixing together well and adding a little more pasta cooking water, if necessary. Cook over a medium-high heat for a minute or so until well combined.

Remove from the heat and serve immediately.

TORTELLI AL MAGRO

Tortelli filled with Swiss chard

In the Italian kitchen, *al magro* refers to dishes that are made simply and without any meat. *Al magro* dishes were popular to eat on Fridays and during Lent when meat was forbidden for religious reasons; some families still observe this rule today. A filled pasta with local greens and cheese, like this one, which is a classic dish of northern Italy, would have been considered such a dish, as it is made with a few readily available ingredients.

I like the taste of Swiss chard and it works really well in this recipe, but you could also use spinach. These tortelli are a half-moon shape, but you could make them into square ravioli or whatever filled pasta shape you like. Served with a rich, butter and sage sauce, these moreish parcels of pasta are a delight.

Serves 4 (makes about 30 tortelli)

For the pasta dough
200g (7oz) '00' pasta flour, plus extra
  for dusting
2 eggs

For the filling
400g (14oz) Swiss chard
drizzle of extra virgin olive oil
1 garlic clove, lightly crushed and left whole
100g (3½oz) fresh ricotta, drained
25g (1oz) grated Parmesan cheese, plus
  extra to serve
1 egg
sea salt and freshly ground black pepper

For the sauce
100g (3½oz) butter
8 sage leaves

continues overleaf

First make the pasta dough. Place the flour in a mixing bowl or in a heap on a clean work surface, make a well in the centre and break in the eggs. Using a fork, gradually mix the flour and eggs together, then knead with your hands to make a smooth dough. Shape into a ball, wrap in clingfilm and leave to rest in the fridge for about 30 minutes or until required.

In the meantime, prepare the filling. Bring a saucepan of water to the boil. Remove the stalks from the Swiss chard (keep them for use in another recipe). Add the green leaves to the pan of boiling water and cook for about 5 minutes, then drain well.

Heat a drizzle of olive oil in a frying pan, sweat the garlic over a medium heat for a minute, then add the drained Swiss chard and stir-fry for a couple of minutes.

Remove from the heat, discard the garlic clove, then leave the Swiss chard to cool. Once cooled, drain, then use your hands to squeeze out the excess liquid. Finely chop the Swiss chard and combine it with the ricotta, grated Parmesan, egg and a little salt and pepper. Set aside.

On a lightly floured work surface, roll out the pasta dough until it is wafer-thin or use a pasta machine on the thinnest setting. Cut out 8cm (4¼in.) circles of dough using a round pastry cutter (about 30 rounds). Place dollops of the filling in the centre of each round, brush the outer edge of each with a little water, then fold over to make a half-moon shape, press to seal and make light indentions with a fork.

Bring a large saucepan of salted water to the boil, then add the tortelli and cook for about 5 minutes until cooked through – try one!

At the same time, for the sauce, melt the butter in a large frying pan over a medium heat, then add the sage leaves and cook until the butter has melted and the leaves are bubbling. Using a slotted spoon, remove the tortelli from the boiling water, add to the melted sage butter and gently mix together.

Remove from the heat and serve with a sprinkling of grated Parmesan.

PASTA AL FORNO CON MELANZANE

Aubergine pasta bake

Baked pasta dishes are very popular in Italy and they are a great way of not only using up leftover ingredients, but also enriching pasta dishes and making them go further. Baked pasta dishes can be elaborate like some lasagne recipes, but can also be quick and simple like this one made with aubergines and tomato sauce.

Serves 4

2 tbsp extra virgin olive oil
2 garlic cloves, lightly crushed and left whole
2 basil stalks, roughly chopped
600ml (1 pint) tomato passata
abundant vegetable oil, for frying
500g (1lb 2oz) aubergines, cut into
  small cubes

300g (10½oz) dried fusilli or spirali pasta
handful of basil leaves
1 ball of mozzarella cheese (about
  125g/4½oz), drained and roughly chopped
70g (2½oz) grated Parmesan cheese
sea salt

Heat the olive oil in a saucepan, add the garlic cloves and basil stalks and sweat over a medium heat for a minute or so. Add the tomato passata and a little salt to taste and cook over a medium-low heat for about 30 minutes.

Preheat the oven to 180°C fan/200°C/gas mark 6.

While the sauce is bubbling away, heat plenty of vegetable oil in a large, deep frying pan until hot, then add some of the aubergine cubes and deep-fry over a medium-to-high heat until golden brown, about 5 minutes. You'll need to deep-fry the aubergine in batches, ensuring you reheat the oil between each batch. Remove each batch using a slotted spoon and leave to drain on kitchen paper.

Meanwhile, cook the pasta in a pan of salted boiling water according to the packet instructions until al dente. Drain well and set aside.

Remove and discard the garlic cloves from the tomato sauce. Combine the remaining tomato sauce with the deep-fried aubergines, the cooked pasta, basil leaves, three-quarters of the mozzarella and half the grated Parmesan.

Pour the mixture into the ovenproof dish, then top with the remaining mozzarella and grated Parmesan. Bake in the oven for about 20–25 minutes until golden brown. Remove from the oven and leave to rest for 5 minutes before serving.

SAGNE E FAGIOLI ALLA CIOCIARA

Pasta with beans from Ciociara

This hearty rural dish is an ancient recipe from Ciociara, the once-impoverished area southeast of Rome. It's a dish that each family makes in their own way and can also be eaten in local restaurants. There are many variations, but it's always made with a simple homemade pasta made of flour and water and local cannellini beans. If you don't want to make your own pasta, you can buy non-egg pappardelle and cut them into smaller shapes. Also, if you don't have much time, you can use 400g (14oz) canned (drained weight) cannellini beans instead of dried.

Serves 4

For the beans
250g (9oz) dried cannellini beans, soaked overnight in plenty of cold water (2 x 400g (14oz) cans cannellini beans)
3 tbsp extra virgin olive oil, plus extra for drizzling
100g (3½oz) pancetta, finely chopped
1 garlic clove, crushed
1 rosemary sprig
sea salt and freshly ground black pepper

For the pasta
300g (10½oz) '00' pasta flour, plus extra for rolling out
approx. 270ml (9½fl oz) water

Drain and rinse the soaked cannellini beans, then cook them in a large saucepan with plenty of fresh water until tender, about 40 minutes – check the instructions on your bean packet.

In the meantime, make the pasta. Place the flour in a large bowl, gradually add the water, mixing to make a smooth dough, then form into a ball and leave to rest at room temperature for about 20 minutes. On a lightly floured work surface, roll out the dough as thinly as you can into a roughly rectangular shape. Cut into 3mm (⅛in.) thick strips, then into small squares, rectangles or diamond shapes roughly 3cm (1¼in.) in length. Set aside.

Finish the beans. Heat the olive oil in a large, deep frying pan, add the pancetta and garlic and sweat over a medium heat for about 5 minutes until the pancetta is golden. Drain the cooked beans and stir them in with a little of the cooking water, the rosemary and some salt and pepper to taste, then cook over a medium heat for a couple of minutes to allow the flavours to infuse.

In the meantime, cook the pasta shapes in a large pan of salted boiling water until they rise to the top, about 1 minute. Remove and drain the pasta with a slotted spoon and add to the beans. Increase the heat, mix well together and cook for a minute or so to allow the flavours to infuse.

Remove from the heat, discard the rosemary stalk, and serve immediately with a drizzle of olive oil and some extra black pepper.

PASTA AL CAVOLFIORE AL FORNO

Baked pasta with cauliflower

This simple but tasty pasta bake is a great way of making cauliflower go further. You could even try using broccoli or Romanesco, if you prefer or have these ingredients to hand. To make it vegetarian, simply omit the ham, and if you have any other cheese you want to use up, just add to the dish, but make sure all the cheeses you use are suitable for vegetarians.

Serves 4

3 tbsp extra virgin olive oil
2 garlic cloves, lightly crushed and left whole
500g (1lb 2oz) cauliflower florets
approx. 300ml (10fl oz) hot water
250g (9oz) dried sedani pasta or pennette
20g (¾oz) butter, plus extra for greasing
60g (2¼oz) grated Parmesan cheese

1 ball of mozzarella cheese (about 125g/4½oz), drained and roughly chopped
50g (1¾oz) cooked ham, finely chopped
15g (½oz) breadcrumbs (fresh, dried or stale)
sea salt and freshly ground black pepper

Preheat the oven to 180°C fan/200°C/gas mark 6. Grease an ovenproof dish with some butter.

Heat the olive oil in a large, deep frying pan, add the garlic and sweat over a medium heat for a minute, then stir in the cauliflower florets and cook for a couple of minutes. Add enough hot water to just about cover the cauliflower, then cover with a lid and cook for 15–20 minutes until tender.

Mash the cauliflower lightly with a fork, but not too much as you still want a bit of bite from the cauliflower. Add salt and pepper to taste, then add a little more hot water and the pasta and cook over a medium heat until the pasta is cooked according to packet instructions. You may need to add a little more hot water – I used a total of 640ml (22fl oz), but you may need more or less depending on the brand of pasta.

When the pasta is cooked, remove the pan from the heat, stir in the butter, 50g (1¾oz) of the grated Parmesan, three-quarters of the mozzarella and all the ham. Pour the pasta mixture into a greased ovenproof dish, then top with the remaining mozzarella and grated Parmesan and the breadcrumbs.

Bake in the oven for about 30 minutes until the top is golden and crispy. Remove from the oven and leave to rest for 5 minutes before serving.

PASTA CON LE CASTAGNE E CECI

Pasta with chestnuts and chickpeas

Years ago in Italy, and certainly when I was a child, chestnuts were enjoyed during the winter season. They were not only eaten by themselves as a nutritious snack, but were also made into delicious recipes as well as ground into flour. Chestnuts were once considered 'food of the poor' because they were easily obtainable and highly nutritious.

For an extra rustic flavour I have combined cooked chestnuts with chickpeas in this hearty pasta dish. You can buy ready-cooked vacuum-packed chestnuts, but I prefer to buy them raw during the season (not only fresher but kinder on your purse!) and either boil them with a couple of bay leaves or roast them in a hot oven before peeling them to add to this recipe. The anchovies add saltiness, but please omit if you're vegetarian.

Serves 4
2 tbsp extra virgin olive oil
2 garlic cloves, lightly crushed and left whole
2 anchovy fillets (optional)
1 red chilli, finely chopped
2 rosemary sprigs, needles stripped and finely chopped
140g (5oz) cooked, peeled chestnuts, roughly chopped
2 x 400g (14oz) cans chickpeas, including their liquid
300g (10½oz) dried gnocchetti (or orecchiette pasta)
approx. 1 litre (1¾ pints) vegetable stock

Heat the olive oil in a large, deep frying pan, add the garlic, anchovy fillets, chilli (if using) and rosemary and sweat over a medium heat for a minute or so. Stir in the chestnuts, followed by the chickpeas and their liquid and cook for a minute.

Stir in the pasta and stock (you may need more or less liquid, so add this gradually – as you would with risotto), bring to a simmer and cook over a medium heat for about 15 minutes (check the cooking time on the pasta packet) until the pasta is cooked to al dente and the liquid has thickened to a creamy consistency.

Remove from the heat, discard the garlic cloves and serve immediately.

LASAGNE CON SALSICCIA E BROCCOLI

Lasagne with sausage and broccoli

Salsiccie e Broccoli is a popular meal in southern Italy. It is made with pork sausages and local bitter *cime di rape* (rape tops) and is usually served as a main course. I have taken these two beloved ingredients and made them into this nutritious lasagne. Instead of *cime di rape,* which is hard to come by, I have used normal broccoli florets, which are cooked and blended. Simple to prepare, it creates an alternative lasagne and a nutritious meal.

Serves 4

350g (12oz) broccoli florets
3 tbsp extra virgin olive oil
1 garlic clove, lightly crushed and left whole
300g (10½oz) Italian pork sausages
½ onion, finely chopped
approx. 6 dried lasagne sheets
40g (1½oz) grated Parmesan cheese
sea salt and freshly ground black pepper

For the béchamel sauce

40g (1½oz) butter
40g (1½oz) plain flour
500ml (18fl oz) milk
pinch of grated nutmeg
10g (¼oz) grated Parmesan cheese

Preheat the oven to 180°C fan/200°C/gas mark 6.

Cook the broccoli in a pan of salted boiling water until tender, about 5 minutes. Drain, reserving a little of the cooking water.

Heat 2 tablespoons of the olive oil in a frying pan, sweat the garlic over a medium heat for a minute, then add the broccoli and stir-fry for about 5 minutes. Remove from the heat and, using a handheld stick blender, blend with the reserved cooking water until smooth. Set aside.

Remove the skins from the sausages and crumble the meat. Heat the remaining olive oil in a separate frying pan, sweat the onion over a medium heat for about 5 minutes until softened, then stir in the crumbled sausage meat, add a little salt to taste and stir-fry over a medium heat for about 10 minutes, until the sausage meat is golden brown.

In the meantime, make the béchamel sauce. Melt the butter in a small saucepan, take it off the heat and quickly whisk in the flour, then gradually whisk in the milk. Return to the heat and cook over a low heat, whisking, until the sauce begins to thicken slightly. Remove from the heat, add a little salt and pepper, the nutmeg and grated Parmesan.

Line an ovenproof dish with a little béchamel sauce, followed by two lasagne sheets and a layer of broccoli, then sprinkle over some sausage meat, then a little grated Parmesan. Continue making layers like these until you have used up all the ingredients, ending with béchamel sauce and a final sprinkling of grated Parmesan.

Cover with foil and bake in the oven for 30 minutes. Remove the foil and continue to bake for a further 15 minutes until golden and bubbling.

Remove from the oven, leave to rest for 5 minutes and then serve.

PASTA E PISELLI CREMOSI

Creamy pasta with peas

This nutritious one-pot dish is a slightly different take on the traditional *Pasta e Piselli*. Half the peas are blended for a creamier consistency and the uncooked pasta is added raw and cooked a bit like a risotto. Depending on your pasta brand, you may need more or less stock. If you're vegetarian, simply omit the pancetta and sub the Parmesan with a similar vegetarian hard cheese. Quick and simple with very few storecupboard ingredients, I'm sure this will become a firm family favourite.

Serves 4
4 tbsp extra virgin olive oil
1 onion, finely chopped
60g (2¼oz) pancetta, finely chopped
360g (12½oz) frozen peas
approx. 1.5 litres (2⅗ pints) hot vegetable stock
320g (11½oz) dried ditalini or tubetti pasta
50g (1¾oz) grated Parmesan cheese
sea salt and freshly ground black pepper

Heat the olive oil in a large, deep frying pan, add the onion and pancetta and cook over a medium heat for about 4 minutes until the onion is softened and the pancetta is golden. Stir in the peas and cook for a minute. Add a couple of tablespoons of the stock and continue to cook over a medium heat for a couple of minutes until the peas are cooked.

Remove from the heat and pour half of the mixture into a blender, then whizz until smooth. Return the blended mixture to the pan with the whole peas, place over the heat, stir in the pasta and pour in the remaining stock. Bring to the boil and continue to cook over a medium-high heat until the pasta is al dente (check the cooking time on the pasta packet).

Remove from the heat and stir in the grated Parmesan, then check for seasoning and add a little salt and pepper, if required. Serve immediately.

RAGÙ DI LENTICCHIE

Lentil ragù

Lentils are an excellent source of protein and a perfect substitute to the traditional minced meat Bolognese. Simple to prepare with basic storecupboard ingredients, it makes a quick meal at any time. You can also make a larger quantity and freeze it in batches.

Lentil ragù is perfect combined with pasta (like in this recipe) or you can enjoy it on its own with some rustic bread. For best results, use the small brown or green lentils that are widely available and do not require pre-soaking. Please note, I have indicated an approximate amount of stock, and also the cooking time may vary, depending on the brand of lentils you use.

Serves 4

3 tbsp extra virgin olive oil
1 onion, finely chopped
1 celery stick, finely chopped
1 carrot, finely chopped
1 bay leaf
40ml (1½fl oz) any type of red wine
200g (7oz) dried small brown or green
   lentils (rinsed)

1 tablespoon tomato purée
approx. 900ml (31fl oz) hot vegetable stock
small piece of Parmesan rind, whole
   (optional)
400g (14oz) dried tagliatelle, linguine,
   spaghetti or penne
sea salt
grated Parmesan cheese, to serve

Heat the olive oil in a large, deep frying pan, add the onion, celery, carrot and bay leaf and sweat over a medium heat for about 4 minutes until softened. Increase the heat, add the wine and allow it to evaporate, then stir in the lentils. Dilute the tomato purée with a little of the vegetable stock and stir in.

Add enough hot stock to cover the lentils, add the Parmesan rind (if using), partially cover with a lid, reduce the heat to medium-low and cook for about 40 minutes until the lentils are cooked. Check from time to time and add more hot stock, if necessary. Depending on the lentils, you may need more or less cooking time and more or less stock.

Near the end of the cooking time, bring a large pot of salted water to the boil and cook the pasta according to the packet instructions until al dente.

Drain the pasta (reserving a little of the cooking water, if needed), add to the lentil ragù and mix well, then cook over a medium-high heat for a minutes or so to combine, adding a little of the reserved pasta cooking water to loosen the ragù a little more, if necessary.

Remove from the heat and serve immediately with a sprinkling of grated Parmesan.

VEGETABLES

PEPERONI RIPIENI

Stuffed peppers

It is so common in Italy and other Mediterranean countries to fill vegetables to make them more nutritious and create a complete meal. Towards the end of summer when peppers are plentiful in Italy, a dish such as this one is very popular, using a filling of leftover bread, ripe plum tomatoes and cheese. For more flavour, I have added pancetta, but if you are vegetarian, please omit and add a little more onion. Serve with a green salad and rustic bread for a delicious meal. The peppers can also be served cold, so they can certainly be made in advance.

Serves 4

4 peppers (any colour)
3 tbsp extra virgin olive oil, plus extra for greasing and drizzling
100g (3½oz) pancetta, finely chopped
1 small onion, finely chopped
300g (10½oz) baby plum tomatoes, quartered

140g (5oz) crustless bread, crumbled into small pieces
40g (1½oz) grated Parmesan cheese
50g (1¾oz) provolone cheese, cut into small cubes
8 basil leaves
sea salt and freshly ground black pepper

Preheat the oven to 160°C fan/180°C/gas mark 4. Grease an ovenproof dish large enough to accommodate the four peppers with a little olive oil.

Cut the tops off the peppers (they should resemble little hats) and set aside. Carefully remove and discard the seeds and white membranes inside each one without breaking the peppers.

Heat the olive oil in a frying pan, add the pancetta and onion and sweat over a medium heat for a couple of minutes. Stir in the tomatoes and cook for about 7 minutes until softened. Add the crumbled bread and continue to cook for 2–3 minutes until well absorbed. Remove from the heat and leave to cool.

Once cool, stir in the cheeses, basil leaves and a little salt and pepper to taste. Fill the peppers with this mixture, then place the lids on top. Place the peppers in the prepared ovenproof dish. Drizzle with a little olive oil, then cover with foil and bake in the oven for 40 minutes.

Remove the foil and continue to bake for a further 40 minutes. Halfway through this baking time, carefully turn the peppers round so they turn a golden brown colour all over.

Remove from the oven, leave to rest for 5 minutes, then serve.

POMODORI RIPIENI AL FORNO

Baked stuffed tomatoes

These baked tomatoes, filled with a few basic ingredients, are simplicity at its tastiest. Depending on the size of your tomatoes, you may not need all the mozzarella, so if you have any left over, place a slice on top of the tomatoes during baking after the foil comes off. They can be served as a side dish or as a main meal with some bread and a green salad.

Serves 4
4 large tomatoes
2 balls of mozzarella cheese (each about 125g/4½oz),
  drained and cut into small pieces
8 basil leaves
pinch of dried oregano
100g (3½oz) breadcrumbs (fresh, dried or stale)
drizzle of olive oil, plus extra for greasing
sea salt and freshly ground black pepper

Preheat the oven to 160°C fan/180°C/gas mark 4. Lightly oil an ovenproof dish.

Slice the tomatoes in half widthways and scoop out the insides into a sieve set over a bowl, allowing the liquid to drain away. Combine the drained tomato flesh and seeds with the mozzarella, basil, oregano and breadcrumbs in a bowl, then season with salt and pepper and add a drizzle of olive oil.

Fill the tomato halves with this mixture, then place in the prepared ovenproof dish. Cover with foil and bake in the oven for 15 minutes, then remove the foil and continue to bake for a further 15 minutes until golden and bubbling.

Remove from the oven, leave to rest for 5 minutes, then serve.

ZUCCHINE RIPIENE

Stuffed courgettes

These tasty filled courgettes are made with all your storecupboard favourites! Cooking the courgettes in boiling water first will make them softer and therefore quicker to bake in the oven. Serve two halves of courgette per person with a mixed salad for a nutritious lunch or dinner.

Serves 4

4 medium courgettes (approx. 1kg/2lb 4oz total weight)

150g (5½oz) canned tuna (drained weight)

100g (3½oz) crustless bread, finely chopped

2 garlic cloves, finely diced

50g (1¾oz) pitted black olives, finely chopped

15g (½oz) capers, finely chopped

1 egg

handful of flat-leaf parsley, finely chopped

6 mint leaves, finely chopped

1 tbsp dried breadcrumbs

extra olive oil, for greasing and drizzling

sea salt and freshly ground black pepper

Preheat the oven to 180°C fan/200°C/gas mark 6. Lightly oil an ovenproof dish.

Trim off the ends, then slice the courgettes in half lengthways. Cook in a pan of salted boiling water for 4 minutes, then remove and drain well. Place on kitchen paper and pat dry.

Carefully scoop out the pulp from the centre of each courgette (leaving the shells intact), then squeeze out the excess liquid from the pulp with your hands and place the pulp in a bowl.

Add the tuna, chopped bread, garlic, olives, capers, egg, parsley and mint to the courgette pulp along with a little salt and pepper to taste and stir to combine. Fill the courgette shells with this mixture, dividing it evenly, and then place in the prepared ovenproof dish. Sprinkle evenly with the breadcrumbs and drizzle with a little olive oil.

Bake in the oven for 40 minutes until golden brown and the courgettes are tender and cooked through. Remove from the oven and leave to rest for a couple of minutes before serving.

CIPOLLE RIPIENE

Baked stuffed onions

The combination of mixed herbs and sultanas here enhances the flavour of the pork. They take a little time to prepare, but are really well worth it and make a delicious main course using just a few ingredients.

Serves 4

4 medium onions, each weighing approx.
  270g (9¾oz)
2 tbsp extra-virgin olive oil, plus extra
  for drizzling
200g (7oz) pork mince
2 tbsp chopped mixed herbs, such as
  rosemary, thyme and sage

50g (1¾oz) stale bread, soaked in 75ml
  (4½ tbsp) warm milk for 10 minutes
40g (1½oz) sultanas, soaked in 50ml
  (1.6fl oz) warm water for 20 minutes
2 eggs
100g (3½oz) grated Parmesan cheese
sea salt and freshly ground black pepper

Preheat the oven to 180°C fan/200°C/gas mark 6. Lightly grease an ovenproof dish with olive oil.

Peel the onions, then place them whole in a pan of boiling water and cook for 10 minutes. Transfer to a plate and leave until cool enough to handle, then cut the onions in half widthways, carefully scooping out the central cavity of each, so you end up with four onion 'containers'. Finely chop the onion cavities.

Heat the olive oil in a frying pan, add the chopped onion and pork mince and stir-fry over a medium heat for a couple of minutes until the meat is sealed. Stir in some salt and pepper and the herbs, then reduce the heat, cover with a lid and continue to cook for about 3 minutes. Remove from the heat and leave to cool.

Once the pork mixture has cooled down, drain any excess liquid before stirring in the soaked bread and sultanas, the eggs and the grated Parmesan until combined. Place the onion 'containers' into the prepared ovenproof dish and stuff them with the filling.

Drizzle with olive oil, then cover with foil and bake in the oven for 25 minutes. Remove the foil and continue to bake for a further 15 minutes until the onions have softened and are golden on top.

Remove from the oven and rest for a couple of minutes before serving.

VERZA RIPIENA

Stuffed whole cabbage

This recipe makes use of both the cabbage and minced meat to make both ingredients go further. It takes a little time to prepare, but it really is worth it, served with a simple tomato sauce, it will surely impress your guests.

Serves 4–6

1 Savoy cabbage (approx 1.2kg/2lb 10oz
   total weight)
2 tbsp extra virgin olive oil
1 onion, finely chopped
500g (1lb 2oz) minced pork
3 sage leaves, finely chopped
½ handful of flat-leaf parsley, finely chopped
200g (7oz) salami, finely chopped
1 egg
10g (¼oz) grated Parmesan cheese
pinch of grated nutmeg
approx. 600ml (20fl oz) hot water
sea salt and freshly ground black pepper

For the tomato sauce:

1 tbsp extra virgin olive oil
½ onion, finely chopped
1 x 400g (14oz) can of chopped tomatoes
sea salt and freshly ground black pepper

Firsst make the tomato sauce. Heat the olive oil in a pan and sweat the onion for a couple of minutes over a medium heat until softened. Stir in the canned tomatoes with about half a can of water, some salt and pepper and cook over a medium heat for about 25 minutes.

In the meantime, remove the hard very green outer leaves of the cabbage, then place in a large pot of lightly salted boiling water and cook over a medium-high heat for 20 minutes. If the pot is not large enough, turn the cabbage upside-down halfway through the cooking time.

Carefully remove the cabbage from the water and wrap it in a clean muslin cloth or fine tea towel, then place head-down over a sieve and leave to drain out all the water.

In the meantime, heat the olive oil in a frying pan and sweat the onion over a medium heat for a couple of minutes, then add the pork mince and stir-fry for a further couple of minutes until sealed. Stir in the sage, parsley and salami. Remove from the heat and leave to cool.

Once the pork mixture has cooled, stir in the egg, grated Parmesan, nutmeg and some salt and pepper to taste.

continues overleaf

Take the cabbage and carefully open up all the leaves, one by one. Then, using a small sharp knife, cut out and discard the hard cavity. Spread a little of the pork filling in between each leaf until you have filled them all. Reshape and tie the filled cabbage with kitchen string and wrap tightly in a clean muslin cloth or tea towel. Place in a large pot, add enough hot water to cover, bring to the boil, then reduce the heat to medium, cover with a lid and cook for 45 minutes.

Remove from the heat, carefully unwrap the cloth or tea towel and cut off the kitchen string, then leave the cabbage to rest for 5 minutes before serving. Slice the stuffed cabbage and serve with the hot tomato sauce.

SFORMATO DI ZUCCHINE

Courgette and ricotta bake

A really simple and nutritious main course that can easily be prepared in advance, then baked or reheated when required. Choose a suitable vegetarian-style hard cheese to replace the Parmesan to make it suitable for vegetarians. Serve with a tomato side salad for an easy supper.

Serves 4

extra virgin olive oil, for greasing and drizzling
80g (3oz) fresh, dried or stale breadcrumbs, plus
  extra for coating and 1 tbsp for sprinkling
700g (1lb 9oz) courgettes
80g (3oz) grated Parmesan cheese
250g (9oz) ricotta, well-drained
2 eggs
8 basil leaves, roughly torn
sea salt and freshly ground black pepper

Preheat the oven to 180°C fan/200°C/gas mark 6. Grease an ovenproof dish with a little olive oil, then sprinkle with some breadcrumbs to coat, tapping out the excess.

Trim and coarsely grate the courgettes, then squeeze out as much of the excess juices as you can. Place the grated courgettes in a large bowl and combine with the grated Parmesan, the 80g (3oz) of breadcrumbs, the ricotta, eggs, basil leaves and a little salt and pepper to taste.

Spoon the courgette mixture into the ovenproof dish, sprinkle with the remaining 1 tablespoon of breadcrumbs and drizzle with more olive oil.

Bake in the oven for 30 minutes until golden and crispy on top. Remove from the oven and leave to rest for 5 minutes before serving.

MELANZANE SPACCATE
Aubergines topped with tomato

This typical recipe originating from Salerno is always a favourite during the summer months when aubergines and tomatoes are in abundance. Try to get long, thin aubergines for the best results. You can make them in advance and enjoy later as a side dish or as a main meal served with a green salad and lots of rustic bread. They can be eaten hot or cold.

Serves 2–4

2 long, thin aubergines
3 tbsp extra virgin olive oil
2 garlic cloves, finely chopped
400g (14oz) baby plum tomatoes, sliced
  into quarters
pinch of dried oregano

30g (1oz) capers
20 pitted black olives
½ handful of basil leaves, plus extra
  to garnish
sea salt

Cut the aubergines in half lengthways, then with a small sharp knife, score the flesh of each half several times. Place, skin-side down, on a flat plate and sprinkle over some salt. Cover with another plate, placing a weight on top, then leave to rest for about 1 hour. This will help exude any bitter juices from the aubergines.

After this time, take each aubergine half and rinse the salt off under cold running water, then with your hands, squeeze out all the excess water and dry with kitchen paper.

Heat 2 tablespoons of the olive oil in a frying pan large enough to hold all four aubergine halves. Place the aubergine halves, skin-side down, in the pan and fry over a medium-high heat for about 5 minutes until golden. Turn them over and fry the flesh side until golden brown, about 5 minutes. Transfer to a plate and set aside.

Heat the remaining olive oil in the same frying pan, add the garlic and sweat over a medium heat for a minute, then stir in the tomatoes, a little salt and the oregano. Reduce the heat and cook for about 3 minutes until the tomatoes have softened. Stir in the capers, olives and basil leaves and continue to cook for a couple of minutes.

Move the tomatoes to one side of the frying pan, leaving enough room to return the aubergine halves to the pan, skin-side down, then place equal amounts of the tomato mixture on top of each aubergine half. Reduce the heat, cover with a lid and cook for about 10 minutes until tender and cooked through.

Remove from the heat, garnish with some fresh basil leaves and serve hot, or set aside to cool and enjoy cold.

PARMIGIANA DI ZUCCA

Pumpkin parmigiana

Parmigiana was originally a dish made with aubergines and came from southern Italy, namely Campania and Sicily, where aubergines grow in abundance. This layered baked dish has, over time, become a popular dish worldwide and has evolved to include other vegetables like courgettes, artichokes, Swiss chard and pumpkin. Whereas aubergines are abundant during the summer, pumpkin is plentiful during the colder season, especially in rural locations where this autumnal squash provided necessary nutrition for families and so was used in a variety of dishes. I like to coat the pumpkin slices in egg and fry them (as I do with all other vegetables when making *Parmigiana*). However, if you prefer a lighter version, you could grill or roast the pumpkin slices instead.

Serves 4–6

1 x 1.4kg (3lb 1oz) pumpkin (you need
  approx. 1kg/2lb 4oz prepped weight)
3–4 eggs
plain flour, for dusting
abundant vegetable oil, for deep-frying
2 balls of mozzarella cheese (each about
  125g/4½oz), drained and roughly chopped
75g (2¾oz) grated Parmesan cheese

For the tomato sauce
2 tbsp extra virgin olive oil
1 small onion, finely chopped
3 x 400g (14oz) cans chopped tomatoes
6 basil leaves
sea salt and freshly ground black pepper

First make the tomato sauce. Heat the olive in a saucepan, add the onion and fry over a medium heat for about 5 minutes, then add the tomatoes, basil leaves and some salt to taste. Leave to simmer over a gentle heat for about 25 minutes until thickened.

In the meantime, peel the pumpkin, cut it in half, then into quarters, remove the seeds and then cut into slices about 5mm (¼in.) thick. Lightly beat the eggs in a shallow dish with a little salt and pepper. Dust the pumpkin slices with flour, shaking off the excess, then dip into the beaten egg.

Heat plenty of vegetable oil in a deep frying pan until hot, then add the pumpkin slices (you may need to do this in batches, depending on the size of your pan) and deep-fry for a couple of minutes on each side. Remove using a slotted spoon and drain on kitchen paper to absorb the excess oil.

Meanwhile, preheat the oven to 180°C fan/200°C/gas mark 6.

continues overleaf

Line an ovenproof dish with a little of the tomato sauce, then place some pumpkin slices over the top, sprinkle with a little black pepper, dot around some mozzarella, sprinkle over some grated Parmesan and top with some more tomato sauce. Continue making layers like these until you have finished all the ingredients, ending with a final sprinkling of mozzarella and grated Parmesan.

Cover with foil and bake in the oven for 15 minutes. Remove the foil and continue to bake for a further 15 minutes until the cheese has melted and has taken on a golden brown colour.

Remove from the oven and leave to rest for about 10 minutes before serving.

INSALATA DI CUORE DI CICORIA

Chicory heart salad

This slightly bitter vegetable goes perfectly with a dressing of extra virgin olive oil, lemon juice and anchovies. You can use the leaves when preparing the chicory for *Fave e Cicoria* recipe (see page 38).

Serves 4–6
400g (14oz) chicory hearts
4 tbsp extra virgin olive oil
juice of 1 lemon
4 anchovy fillets, finely chopped
sea salt and freshly ground black pepper

Slice the chicory hearts thinly lengthways and place in a serving dish.

Combine the olive oil, lemon juice, chopped anchovy fillets and some salt and pepper to taste in a small bowl, then pour this over the chicory, toss together well and serve.

POLPETTE DI MELANZANE

Mini aubergine burgers

Aubergines, widely used and grown during the summer in southern Italy, make a perfect alternative to meat. These are usually made into *Polpettine* (small balls), but while testing, I decided to make them into mini burgers for a change – same taste, different shape! If you prefer, you can make them a little larger and serve them in a burger bun with salad leaves and pickles for a delicious meat-free burger.

Makes 8 mini burgers

500g (1lb 2oz) aubergines
50g (1¾oz) crustless bread, soaked in 4½ tbsp of warm water
1 garlic clove, finely diced
10g (¼oz) dried breadcrumbs
20g (¾oz) grated Parmesan cheese
handful of flat-leaf parsley leaves, finely chopped
1 egg
abundant vegetable oil, for frying
sea salt and freshly ground black pepper

Place a large pan of water on to boil. In the meantime, cut the aubergines into small chunks. When the water is boiling, tip the aubergines in and blanch for a couple of minutes, then drain well and leave to dry out and cool on a clean tea towel. Once cool, squeeze out all the excess water from the chunks (this can easily be done by putting the aubergine chunks through a potato ricer, if you have one).

Squeeze the soaked bread to remove the excess water, then roughly chop. Combine the aubergines, bread, garlic, breadcrumbs, grated Parmesan, parsley and egg in a bowl, then season with some salt and pepper to taste. Form the mixture into eight mini burgers, each just under 1cm (½in.) thick.

Heat plenty of vegetable oil in a deep frying pan until hot, then add the burgers (you may need to do this in a couple of batches, depending on the size of your pan) and shallow-fry over a medium-to-high heat for 2–3 minutes on each side until golden. Remove and drain on kitchen paper, then serve immediately.

FRITTELLE DI CAVOLFIORE

Cauliflower fritters

These delicious fritters are very addictive and a great way to use up leftover cooked cauliflower. They are ideal served as a snack or with a mixed salad and some bread for a light lunch or supper.

Makes 8–10 fritters

350g (12oz) cauliflower florets
2 eggs, beaten
50g (1¾oz) grated Parmesan cheese
35g (1¼oz) self-raising flour, sifted
1 garlic clove, finely diced
½ handful of flat-leaf parsley, finely sliced
abundant vegetable oil, for frying
sea salt and freshly ground black pepper

Cook the cauliflower florets in a pan of boiling water for about 6 minutes until tender, then drain, dry on a clean tea towel, place in a bowl and mash with a fork. Leave to cool.

Add the eggs, grated Parmesan, flour, garlic and parsley to the mashed cauliflower, along with some salt and pepper to taste, and mix together well.

Heat plenty of vegetable oil in a deep frying pan until hot, then add large spoonfuls of the cauliflower mixture, flattening each one a little with the back of the spoon. Deep-fry for about 3 minutes on each side until golden (you may need to cook the fritters in a couple of batches, depending on the size of your pan).

Remove and drain well on kitchen paper, then serve hot.

LA CIPOLLATA CON LE UOVA

Slow-cooked onions with eggs

This *cucina povera* dish originating from the Abruzzo region would often be made in rural areas during the onion harvest, sometimes with the addition of tomatoes, and served with rustic bread to mop up the juices. The slow-cooking process of the onions makes them lovely and sweet. To enrich the dish, I have added eggs, which makes a complete and tasty meal at any time using a few economical ingredients. Serve 1 or 2 eggs per person, depending on how hungry you are.

Serves 2–4
5 tbsp extra virgin olive oil
1kg (2lb 4oz) onions, finely sliced
3½ tbsp water
200g (7oz) baby plum tomatoes, cut in half
4 eggs
sea salt and freshly ground black pepper
rustic bread, to serve

Heat the olive oil in a frying pan, add the onions and sweat over a medium-high heat for a minute or so. Add salt and pepper to taste, pour in the water, then reduce the heat to low, cover with a lid and cook gently for 35 minutes.

Add the tomatoes, placing them over the onions around the outer edge of the pan, and continue to cook over a low heat for 15 minutes.

Remove the lid, then, with a wooden spoon, gently make four indents in the onions. Crack an egg into each indent, then cover with a lid and cook gently for about 3–5 minutes until the eggs are cooked to your liking.

Remove from the heat and serve immediately with some good rustic bread.

INSALATA DI RINFORZO

Cauliflower salad

This colourful salad is a must on Christmas Eve tables in most Neapolitan households, and it is traditionally eaten throughout the festive period, adding vegetables and pickles to the bowl until the new year. This tradition dates back to when nothing was ever wasted and whatever vegetables were left over would be put in a jar with home-made vinegar to preserve. These days, apart from the cooked cauliflower, the rest of the vegetables come from ready-prepared pickles.

In Italy, *Giardiniera* is very popular and these ready-made jars of pickled vegetables can be found in good Italian delis. And in Naples, sweet peppers are a must in this salad. However, you can use whatever pickles you prefer and include a variety like peppers, aubergines, carrots, celery, gherkins and/or onions. If you make your own preserved vegetables, even better, but shop-bought ones are just as good and very handy to keep in your storecupboard.

This is my version of this salad, but you can add whatever you like and, as they do in Italy, keep adding to it; you can also add more or less vinegar, depending on taste. It is best made in advance and left to rest overnight in the fridge so all the flavours infuse nicely.

Serves 2–4

½ small red onion, finely sliced
approx. 3 tbsp red wine vinegar
500g (1lb 2oz) cauliflower florets
approx. 200g (7oz) preserved/pickled
  vegetables (to include peppers), drained
10 pitted olives (black or green)

4 sun-dried tomatoes, roughly chopped
6 cornichons, drained and roughly chopped
4 anchovy fillets (optional)
¼ red chilli, finely chopped (optional)
2 tbsp extra virgin olive oil
sea salt

Place the red onion in a small bowl, cover with red wine vinegar and leave to marinate.

Cook the cauliflower florets in a pan of salted boiling water for about 6 minutes or until just tender, but do not allow them to overcook and go mushy. Drain well and leave to cool.

Place the cauliflower florets in a serving bowl together with the drained red onion (reserve the vinegar), preserved/pickled vegetables, olives, sun-dried tomatoes and cornichons, and the anchovy fillets and chilli (if using), and toss together to mix. Drizzle over some or all of the red wine vinegar from the onion, along with the olive oil, and toss lightly. If necessary, add a little salt to taste.

Leave to rest at room temperature for at least a couple of hours before serving, otherwise cover and leave overnight in the fridge, but serve at room temperature.

MEAT AND FISH

SGOMBRO ALLA PIZZAIOLA

Mackerel in pizzaiola sauce

Alla Pizzaiola is the term used to cook meat or fish with tomatoes, capers and oregano. This full-of-flavour sauce works well with fresh mackerel, and makes a quick and easy meal when served with some rustic bread. If you make more sauce, you can serve it with some freshly cooked pasta as a starter and then enjoy the fish as a main course.

Serves 4

2 tbsp extra virgin olive oil
2 garlic cloves, finely chopped
¼ red chilli, finely chopped (optional)
400g (14oz) baby plum tomatoes, halved
20g (¾oz) capers
10 pitted black olives
pinch of dried oregano
handful of flat-leaf parsley, finely chopped
4 mackerel fillets (approx. 500g/1lb 2oz in
  total), skinned or skin-on
2 tbsp warm water
sea salt

Heat the olive oil in a large, deep frying pan, add the garlic and chilli and sweat over a medium heat for a minute. Stir in the tomatoes, capers, olives, oregano, half of the parsley and a little salt and stir-fry over a medium-high heat for a couple of minutes. Reduce the heat, cover with a lid and cook for 5 minutes.

Remove the lid, place the mackerel fillets on top of the sauce, drizzle over the warm water, then cover with a lid again and cook for 5 minutes. Remove the lid, increase the heat and continue to cook for about 2 minutes to evaporate most of the liquid.

Remove from the heat, scatter over the rest of the parsley and serve immediately.

SARDINE MARINATE E FRITTE

Marinated and fried sardines

Sardines have always been economical and thankfully still are. They are popular throughout the coastal areas of Italy, simply grilled, or in Sicily they are used in pasta dishes and filled to make them go further. This recipe marinates the sardines to add flavour before coating them in breadcrumbs and deep-frying. Make sure you ask your fishmonger to remove the heads and guts and butterfly the fish. Delicious served with salad and rustic bread.

Serves 2

6 sardines, heads removed, gutted and butterflied
plain flour, for dusting
1 egg, lightly beaten
Dried breadcrumbs, for coating
abundant vegetable oil, for deep-frying
lemon wedges, to serve

For the marinade
juice of ½ lemon
1 tbsp extra virgin olive oil
1 anchovy fillet, finely chopped
½ handful of flat-leaf parsley, finely chopped

For the gremolata
1 garlic clove, diced
½ handful of flat-leaf parsley, finely chopped
zest of 1 lemon

Combine the marinade ingredients. Place the sardines in a non-metallic dish, pour over the marinade and leave to marinate in the fridge for at least 30 minutes, ideally overnight.

In the meantime, combine all the ingredients for the gremolata in a bowl and set aside.

Remove the sardines from the marinade and pat dry on kitchen paper. Coat the fish in flour, shaking off the excess, then dip in the beaten egg and coat in breadcrumbs.

Heat plenty of vegetable oil in a deep frying pan until hot, then deep-fry the sardines in the oil for a minute or so on each side until golden. Remove and drain on kitchen paper. Serve immediately with a sprinkling of the gremolata and the lemon wedges.

ACCIUGHE IN SALSA VERDE

Anchovies in salsa verde

This traditional Piemontese recipe actually originates from the *cucina povera*, when a green sauce made of herbs, bread and vinegar was added to fresh anchovies to make them go further. These days it is made as an antipasto and can be served on small *crostini* (toasted bread) and/or to accompany cured meats. For maximum flavour, try to get the best canned anchovies you can find. You can also make more and preserve them in a sealed jar.

Serves 4–6
5 tbsp extra virgin olive oil
20g (¾oz) stale bread, soaked in red or
  white wine vinegar, then roughly chopped
1 garlic clove, very finely diced
¼ red chilli, very finely chopped
handful of flat-leaf parsley, very finely
  chopped
2 x 50g (1.7oz) cans anchovies in oil

Combine all the ingredients (except the anchovies) in a bowl to make the salsa verde.

Drain the anchovies of their oil (discard the oil) and arrange them on a serving dish. Spread the salsa verde over the anchovies and leave to rest at room temperature for at least 30 minutes before serving.

If you prefer, you can make layers of the above; layering the anchovies and salsa verde in a sterilized jar, then seal well, store in a cool, dark place and use when required. It will keep in the fridge for up to a week.

INVOLTINI ALLA GENOVESE
Rolled filled pork slow-cooked in onions

La Genovese is a typical Neapolitan dish of slow-cooked meat with lots of onions. There are many theories as to why this Neapolitan dish is called *Genovese* and one is that a dish of meat and onions was made by sailors from Genova when docking in Naples. Another is that it was made by a Neapolitan chef called O'Genovese. Whichever is correct or not, the dish has nothing to do with the Ligurian town of Genova and is 100 per cent Neapolitan.

The large amount of onions probably masked the flavour of cheaper cuts of meat and was served with pasta to make the dish go further. Nowadays, this dish is made with veal, pork or beef, and during cooking, the onions exude a lot of liquid and melt down to gooey deliciousness. My version is with pork *involtini* – pork loin slices that are filled and rolled, then cooked in the onions. You can enjoy this dish as a main course with lots of good rustic bread, or you could mix the onion sauce with freshly cooked pasta, such as penne, and then the pork *involtini*.

Serves 4

8 slices of pork loin, approx. 750g (1lb 10oz) in total
½ handful of flat-leaf parsley, finely chopped
2 garlic cloves, finely chopped
15g (½oz) grated Parmesan cheese
3 tbsp extra virgin olive oil
1kg (2lb 4oz) onions, finely sliced
½ celery stick, finely chopped
1 small carrot, finely chopped
1 bay leaf
1 rosemary sprig
100ml (3½fl oz) white wine
sea salt and freshly ground black pepper
rustic bread, to serve

Bash the slices of pork between two pieces of clingfilm to make them thinner, then set aside on a chopping board.

Combine the parsley, garlic and grated Parmesan with a little salt and pepper in a bowl, then place a spoonful on each of the pork slices. Carefully roll up each slice with the filling inside, then secure each one with a cocktail stick. These are your *involtini*.

Heat 1 tablespoon of olive oil in a large, deep frying pan over a medium-to-high heat, add the *involtini* and seal well all over, about 10 minutes until golden brown. Transfer to a plate and set aside.

Heat the remaining olive oil in the same pan, add the onions, celery, carrot, bay leaf, rosemary and a little salt and pepper and stir-fry over a medium-high heat for 5 minutes. Add the white wine, return the *involtini* to the pan, reduce the heat, cover with a lid and cook gently for 2½ hours. If you find there is still a lot of liquid towards the end

of the cooking time, remove the lid and cook over a medium-high heat for a few minutes until most of the liquid has evaporated.

Remove from the heat, discard the bay leaf and rosemary stalk and serve the pork *involtini* with the onion sauce and lots of good rustic bread.

FRICCO' DI POLLO ALL'ARRABBIATA

Chicken with spicy tomato sauce

This rustic chicken dish from Umbria is a great way of using up tomatoes that are just a bit too ripe for salads. The combination of garlic, chilli and the essential oils that exude from the finely chopped rosemary complement this dish perfectly. Simple to prepare with just a few ingredients, I'm sure this will be your go-to chicken dish. Serve with good, rustic bread to mop up the delicious juices.

Serves 4

1kg (2lb 4oz) chicken pieces on the bone, such as
  thighs and drumsticks (either skin-on or skinless)
3 tbsp extra virgin olive oil
3 garlic cloves, lightly crushed and left whole
1 red chilli, finely chopped
2 tbsp finely chopped rosemary needles
150ml (5fl oz) white wine
500g (1lb 2oz) ripe cherry or baby plum tomatoes,
  cut in half (or any ripe tomatoes you have)
sea salt and freshly ground black pepper
rustic bread, to serve

Heat the oil in a large frying pan over a high heat, add the chicken pieces, then reduce the heat to medium and cook the chicken on all sides to seal, about 15 minutes. Cover with a lid and cook for a further couple of minutes. Transfer the chicken to a plate and set aside. Discard any fat remaining in the pan.

Return the pan to the heat, add a little more olive oil, then sweat the garlic, chilli and rosemary over a gentle heat for a minute or so. Return the chicken pieces to the pan, add some salt and pepper, then increase the heat, add the wine and allow it to evaporate. Reduce the heat again, stir in the tomatoes, cover with a lid and cook over a gentle heat for
30 minutes until the chicken is cooked through.

Serve immediately with lots of good rustic bread.

MONDEGHILI

Beef meatballs

These delicious meatballs originate from the Milanese region of Lombardy in the days when nothing was wasted and are made from leftover boiled or roast beef and bread. The name *Mondeghili* in the regional dialect simply means polpette or meatballs. Nowadays, mortadella, salami or even sausage meat can be added for extra flavour. You can, of course, make them with any leftover boiled or roasted meat, so they're perfect for when you have Sunday lunch leftovers.

Be careful when cooking these meatballs, as the butter can turn brown very quickly, so keep the heat fairly low and, if necessary, add a little more extra virgin olive oil. Delicious served with some mashed potato and greens or simply with a green salad.

Serves 4 (makes approx. 16 meatballs)

300g (10½oz) boiled beef (see Bollito di Manzo recipe on page 154)
130g (4¾oz) stale bread, soaked in milk
75g (2¾oz) mortadella or Milano salami, finely chopped
25g (1oz) grated Parmesan cheese
zest of ½ lemon
1 garlic clove, finely diced
pinch of grated nutmeg
2 eggs
dried breadcrumbs, for coating
70g (2½oz) butter
1 tbsp extra virgin olive oil
sea salt and freshly ground black pepper

Using a sharp knife, very finely chop the cooked beef. Take the soaked bread and squeeze it well between your hands, discarding the excess milk. Combine the beef with the bread, mortadella or salami, grated Parmesan, lemon zest, garlic, nutmeg, eggs and some salt and pepper to taste.

Form the mixture into about 16 meatballs, each about the size of a golf ball, then with your hand, squash each one a little and then coat all over in breadcrumbs. Place on a plate and leave to rest in the fridge for about 30 minutes.

Heat the butter and olive oil in a large frying pan over a medium heat, then add the meatballs and fry over a medium-low heat for about 2–3 minutes on each side, until cooked and lightly browned all over. You may have to do this in a couple of batches, depending on the size of your frying pan.

Remove from the pan and leave to drain on kitchen paper for a couple of minutes, then serve.

TRIPPA CON FAGIOLI

Tripe with beans

Although often frowned upon, I love tripe! I used to eat it during my childhood and I still cook it today. What a treat it is! It has always been economical as it was this part of the animal that was discarded by the nobles and left for the poor who came up with ingenious ways of cooking it. Over time, tripe has become part of Italian cuisine and a trip to Florence would not be complete without trying a plate of *Trippa alla Fiorentina* or the street food version, *Lampredotto*, served in a bread bun.

But tripe is not only popular in Tuscany. Throughout Italy, tripe is cooked in a variety of ways and, although it may not be enjoyed by everyone, it's an excellent and economical source of protein. This is my version cooked with pancetta, tomatoes and cannellini beans for extra nutrition and flavour. Serve with lots of good toasted bread for a hearty meal.

Serves 4

650g (1lb 7oz) beef tripe, cut into 5cm
  (2in.) strips
4 tbsp white wine vinegar
4 tbsp extra virgin olive oil
100g (3½oz) pancetta, cut into small cubes
1 onion, finely chopped
1 celery stick, finely chopped
1 carrot, finely chopped
1 garlic clove, finely chopped
1 red chilli, finely chopped
3 bay leaves

100ml (3½fl oz) white wine
1 x 400g (14oz) can chopped tomatoes
handful of basil leaves, roughly torn
1 x 400g (14oz) can cannellini beans,
  including their liquid
sea salt

To serve
grated Parmesan cheese
slices of toasted rustic bread, drizzled with
  extra virgin olive oil

Place the tripe in a saucepan of water with the vinegar, bring to the boil and cook for 5 minutes.

In the meantime, heat the olive oil in a large, deep frying pan, add the pancetta, onion, celery, carrot, garlic, chilli and bay leaves and sweat over a medium heat for 2–3 minutes.

Drain the tripe and stir it into the onion mixture, then increase the heat, add the wine and allow it to evaporate. Add the tomatoes, basil and a little salt and cook, covered with a lid, over a medium-low heat for 30 minutes. Stir in the cannellini beans including their liquid and cook for a further 5 minutes.

Remove from the heat, discard the bay leaves and then serve immediately with a sprinkling of grated Parmesan and slices of oil-drizzled toasted bread.

SPEZZATINO DI COLLO D'AGNELLO

Neck of lamb stew

Neck of lamb is an economical cut of meat and ideal for slow-cooked stews such as this one. Ask your butcher for slices of lamb neck as these will make it quicker and easier to cook. Lamb has always been a popular meat in rural areas in central and southern Italy and, with the addition of potatoes here, makes a lovely one-pot meal. The potatoes help the liquid to thicken nicely without the need to add any thickening agents. Serve with lots of good rustic bread to mop up the juices.

Serves 4
4 slices of lamb neck (approx. 800g/1lb 12oz total weight)
plain flour, for dusting
4 tbsp extra virgin olive oil
2 anchovy fillets
2 onions, cut into quarters
2 large carrots, cut into chunks
8 thyme sprigs
900ml (31fl oz) chicken stock
500g (1lb 2oz) potatoes, peeled and cut into chunks
rustic bread, to serve

Coat the lamb slices in flour, shaking off any excess. Heat the olive oil in a large sauté pan, add the anchovy fillets and lamb and cook over a medium heat until the lamb is sealed and the anchovy fillets have dissolved, about 10 minutes. Transfer the lamb to a plate and set aside.

In the same pan, add the onions and sweat over a medium heat for a couple of minutes. Stir in the carrots and thyme and continue to cook for a minute. Return the lamb to the pan, placing it over the vegetables. Pour over the stock, bring to the boil, then reduce the heat, partially cover with a lid and cook gently for 1 hour 20 minutes.

After this time, add the potatoes and continue to cook without the lid for a further 25 minutes until the potatoes are cooked and the liquid has thickened slightly.

Remove from the heat and serve immediately with lots of rustic bread.

POLPETTONE CON UOVA, PROSCIUTTO E PROVOLONE CON PATATE ARROSTO

Meatloaf with eggs, ham and provolone cheese served with baby roast potatoes

Polpettone is a good way of making minced meat go further and using up any leftovers of ham or cheese. The addition of eggs enriches the dish even more. Serve with roasted baby potatoes for a tasty and nutritious meal.

Serves 4

70g (2½oz) crustless stale bread, cut into small chunks
100ml (3½fl oz) milk
4 eggs
200g (7oz) beef mince
200g (7oz) pork mince
30g (1oz) grated Parmesan cheese
½ handful of flat-leaf parsley, finely chopped
1 garlic clove, diced
60g (2¼oz) cooked ham

30g (1oz) provolone cheese, cut into thin slices
65ml (2fl oz) water
½ tbsp plain flour
dried breadcrumbs, for coating
500g (1lb 2oz) baby potatoes
2 garlic cloves, lightly crushed and left whole
thyme and rosemary sprigs, a couple of each
extra virgin olive oil, for drizzling
sea salt and freshly ground black pepper

Soak the bread in the milk for about 20 minutes until softened. Squeeze out if necessary.

In the meantime, cook three of the eggs in a pan of boiling water for about 8–10 minutes until they are hard-boiled. Remove from the heat, drain and then place in cold water and leave to cool. Once cool, remove the shells.

Combine the beef and pork mince, the softened bread, the remaining egg, the Parmesan, parsley, diced garlic and a little salt and pepper in a bowl.

Place a large sheet of clingfilm on the work surface and place the meat mixture on top, spreading it into a roughly flat rectangular shape, approx. 28 x 20cm (11 x 8in.). Lay the ham slices over the top, then the provolone slices and top with the whole hard-boiled eggs. Carefully roll up with the help of the clingfilm into a large sausage shape, securing well at the ends and pressing all over to avoid any holes or gaps. Leave to rest in the fridge for 30 minutes.

Preheat the oven to 200°C fan/220°C/gas mark 7. Line a 900g (2lb) loaf tin with baking paper or a baking paper loaf liner.

Make a smooth liquid paste using the water and flour, then set aside.

Carefully remove and discard the clingfilm from the meatloaf. Coat the meatloaf all over with the liquid flour paste and then coat in breadcrumbs. Carefully place the meatloaf into the lined loaf tin, reshaping it a little to fit the tin. Bake in the oven for 55 minutes until cooked through and lightly browned.

Meanwhile, place the baby potatoes in a roasting tin with the whole crushed garlic cloves, the herb sprigs, a little salt and pepper and a drizzle of olive oil and toss to mix well. Place in the oven about 15 minutes after the meatloaf has gone in. Once ready, the potatoes will be golden brown and crispy.

Remove both from the oven, carefully take the meatloaf out of the tin, discard the lining paper or liner and place on a plate. Slice and serve with the roasted baby potatoes.

BOLLITO DI MANZO E PASTINA IN BRODO

Boiled beef with pastina in broth

Bollito can be made with a variety of meats like beef, chicken and veal. The broth is eaten as a starter with some *pastina* (small pasta shapes), or small meat ravioli are added. The meats are then eaten as a main course. Of course, *Bollito* was not always this elaborate and it enabled people to use cheaper cuts of meat to make just as good a meal. I've used beef skirt, which is economical, and with the addition of bone is excellent for making broth. Any leftover beef can be used to make *Mondeghili* meatballs, page 148.

Serves 4

1.1kg (2lb 6oz) beef skirt on the bone
2 onions, cut in half
2 celery sticks, cut in half
2 large carrots, cut in half
handful of flat-leaf parsley, including the
*   stalks*
approx. 600ml (20fl oz) hot water
2 x 28g (1oz) light beef or vegetable stock pots

200g (7oz) dried pastina, i.e. stelline,
*   farfalline, risoni, alphabet or broken-up*
*   spaghetti*

To serve
freshly ground black pepper
grated Parmesan cheese

Place the beef in a large saucepan, cover with enough water to come about 2.5cm (1in.) above the meat, then bring to the boil and boil for 10 minutes. Transfer the meat to a plate and discard the water.

Return the meat to the saucepan along with the vegetables and parsley, cover with enough hot water to come about 2.5cm (1in.) above the meat, then add the stock pots. Bring to the boil, then reduce the heat, cover with a lid and cook gently for about 2 hours until the meat is really tender.

Transfer the meat and vegetables (use a slotted spoon for the veg) from the pan to a dish and keep warm. Strain the stock and return it to the pan, then bring back to the boil. Add the *pastina*, reduce the heat and cook until the *pastina* is ready, about 7 minutes (check the cooking times on your packet).

Serve the *pastina* broth with a sprinkling of black pepper and grated Parmesan as a starter, followed by the sliced meat and vegetables as a main course.

Cook's Tip
With the above quantities, you should make approx. 1.2–1.3 litres (2–2¼ pints) of broth.

BRODO DI POLLO
Chicken broth

In Italy, to produce the best broth, an older hen, known as *gallina*, is used. Ask your butcher for an older boiling chicken, otherwise a normal roasting one will be fine. However, to enhance the flavour, I always like to add a couple of chicken stock pots. There is nothing more comforting than a bowl of hot steaming chicken broth perhaps with the addition of some *pastina* (small pasta shapes) followed by the boiled chicken and vegetables. Use the broth for the *Passatelli in Brodo* recipe (see page 45). The chicken is also delicious eaten cold in a salad with a drizzle of extra virgin olive oil and balsamic vinegar. And if you have leftover broth, simply freeze it for another time.

Serves 4
1.2kg (2lb 10oz) chicken
1 large onion, cut into quarters
2 celery sticks, including leaves, cut in half
2 large carrots
handful of parsley, including the stalks
2 x 28g (1oz) chicken stock pots
sea salt (optional)

Place all the ingredients, except the salt, in a large saucepan and add enough water to cover the chicken. Bring to the boil, then reduce the heat, cover with a lid and simmer gently for about 1½ hours until the chicken is cooked through.

Transfer the chicken and vegetables to a bowl and set aside. Strain the liquid through a fine sieve, then season with a little salt, if necessary.

You can use this clear broth as a soup by adding some small pasta shapes and simmering until cooked, or use it for the *Passatelli in Brodo* recipe (see page 45). Or shred the chicken and chop the cooked vegetables and add back into the broth, then reheat before serving, for a more substantial soup.

POLLO IN SCAPECE

Chicken in vinegar and mint

In Scapece is a Neapolitan term to mean food that is marinated in vinegar and mint, like the popular *Zucchine alla Scapece*. Although not marinated in vinegar, the chicken has a lovely subtle vinegar taste. For a richer flavour, make this dish the day before, store in the fridge and then serve it at room temperature.

Serves 4
4 tbsp extra virgin olive oil
1kg (2lb 4oz) mixed chicken thighs and legs
* (bone-in and either skin-on or skinless)*
125ml (4fl oz) white wine
1 onion, finely sliced
3 carrots, sliced
4 garlic cloves, lightly crushed and left whole
½ red chilli, finely chopped
125ml (4fl oz) white wine vinegar
200g (7oz) baby plum tomatoes, halved
handful of mint leaves
2 bay leaves
approx. 400ml (13½fl oz) hot water
sea salt and freshly ground black pepper

Heat the olive oil in a large frying pan over a medium-high heat, add the chicken pieces and seal very well all over, about 15 minutes. Transfer the chicken pieces to a plate.

Add the wine to the pan and deglaze, stirring to release all the tasty bits on the bottom of the pan. Stir in the onion, carrot, garlic, chilli and some salt and pepper and cook over a gentle heat for 10 minutes.

Return the chicken pieces to the pan, add the vinegar, tomatoes, mint and bay leaves, then add enough hot water to cover. Partially cover with a lid and cook over a gentle heat for about 30 minutes until the chicken is cooked through.

Remove from the heat and leave to rest for 20 minutes before serving. Or this dish can be enjoyed cold (see intro). Discard the bay leaves before serving.

MERLUZZO E PATATE AL FORNO

Baked white fish and potatoes

Fish and potatoes always go well together and in Italy we would often have *Baccalà e Patate* (salt cod and potatoes.) Salt fish was always good value and kept for long periods of time. Sadly, over time, *Baccalà* has increased in price and is no longer the *cucina povera* ingredient it once was. So, instead I have come up with this simple baked fish and potato dish enhanced with a tasty breadcrumb mixture. Quick and easy to prepare, use whatever good white fish you find at your fishmonger, for a nutritious meal.

Serves 4
50g (1¾oz) breadcrumbs (fresh, dried or stale)
handful of flat-leaf parsley leaves, finely chopped
1 garlic clove, finely diced
zest of ½ lemon
500g (1lb 2oz) potatoes
extra virgin olive oil, for drizzling
2 tbsp water
4 skin-on white fish fillets (such as cod or whiting), each about 150g (5oz)
sea salt and freshly ground black pepper

Preheat the oven to 180°C fan/200°C/gas mark 6.

Combine the breadcrumbs, parsley, garlic and lemon zest in a bowl and set aside.

Peel the potatoes and cut into 3mm (⅛in.) thick slices. Drizzle a little olive oil into an ovenproof dish, place a layer of half the potato slices in the dish, then sprinkle with a little salt and pepper. Sprinkle about a third of the breadcrumb mixture over the top, followed by a drizzle of olive oil. Repeat to make another layer like the first one, ensuring you keep the remaining breadcrumb mixture for later. Spoon the water around the sides, then cover with foil and bake in the oven for 30 minutes. Remove the foil and continue to bake for a further 10 minutes.

Place the fish fillets, skin-side down, over the potatoes, sprinkle with the remaining breadcrumb mixture, then drizzle with olive oil and bake for a further 17 minutes until the fish is cooked through.

Remove from the oven and serve with either a side of steamed greens or a green salad.

PANADINE SARDE

Sardinian mini meat pies

These savoury pies originate from Sardinia and were often made with leftover bread dough enriched with lard and filled with whatever ingredients were available. Minced meat and/or vegetables are a popular filling these days and I have used lamb in my recipe. But you can, of course, use beef or pork mince or a mixture of the two, or you can use whatever vegetables you have to hand or want to use up, if you prefer. Serve with a green or mixed salad for a complete meal. These mini pies are also perfect to take on picnics or for a packed lunch.

Makes 10 mini pies

For the pastry
400g (14oz) '00' pasta flour, plus extra
  for dusting
pinch of sea salt
150g (5½oz) chilled butter
approx. 150ml (5fl oz) water

For the filling
2 tsp extra virgin olive oil
1 small onion, finely chopped

200g (7oz) lamb mince
8 mint leaves, roughly torn
30ml (1fl oz) white wine
180g (6¼oz) potatoes, peeled and cut into
  small cubes
100g (3½oz) frozen peas
15g (½oz) grated pecorino cheese
1 egg yolk, beaten with a splash of milk
sea salt and freshly ground black pepper

First make the pastry. Combine the flour and salt in a large bowl, cut the butter into small chunks, add to the bowl and then use your fingertips to work the flour and butter together until the mixture resembles breadcrumbs. Gradually add enough cold water, mixing to make a smooth pastry. Form the pastry into a ball, wrap in clingfilm and leave to rest in the fridge for at least 30 minutes while you get on with making the filling.

To make the filling, heat the olive oil in a frying pan, add the onion and sweat over a medium heat for about 3 minutes until softened. Stir in the lamb mince and cook until well sealed all over, about 7 minutes. Add the mint leaves and some salt and pepper, then add the wine and cook for about 5 minutes. Add the potatoes, cover with a lid and cook for about 10 minutes, then add the peas and cook for a further 2 minutes until the potatoes are just tender. Remove from the heat, leave the mixture to cool, then stir in the pecorino.

Preheat the oven to 180°C fan/200°C/gas mark 6. Line a baking sheet with baking paper.

Roll out the pastry on a lightly floured work surface to about 5mm (¼in.) thickness. Cut out 10 circles using a 10cm (4in.) round pastry cutter and then cut out 10 more circles using a 9cm (3½in.) round pastry cutter, re-rolling the trimmings, if necessary.

Take one of the larger pastry circles in the palm of your hand and fill with 3–4 teaspoons of the lamb mixture. Place a smaller pastry circle over the top, pressing it down well around the edges so the filling doesn't escape. With your fingers, crimp the edges. Repeat with the remaining pastry circles and filling to make 10 pies in total. Place the pies on the lined baking sheet and brush all over with the egg wash. Bake in the oven for 40 minutes until golden brown.

Remove from the oven and serve hot or cold. If serving cold, these pies will keep in an airtight container in the fridge for up to 3 days.

RAGÙ DI STINCO DI MAIALE

Pork knuckle ragù

Pork knuckle is an economic cut of meat and ideal for slow cooking in a ragù. For extra flavour, I have seasoned the pork with a mix of garlic, herbs and grated Parmesan. Pork knuckle takes time to cook, but the resulting rich tomato sauce can be served with some freshly cooked pasta and the pork enjoyed as a main course with a green salad. Any leftover tomato sauce can be stored in the fridge or freezer for another time. As is typical in Italian meat ragù, this simple effortless dish can be enjoyed for two courses and in Italy is usually served for Sunday lunch.

Serves 4

2 garlic cloves, diced

2 rosemary sprigs, needles stripped and finely chopped

handful of flat-leaf parsley, finely chopped

zest of ¼ lemon

10g (¼oz) grated Parmesan cheese

1.5kg (3lb 5oz) pork knuckle (in one piece)

5 tbsp extra virgin olive oil

50ml (2fl oz) white wine

½ onion, finely chopped

1 celery stick, finely chopped

1 small carrot, finely chopped

1 litre (1¾ pints) tomato passata

approx. 600ml (20fl oz) water

sea salt and freshly ground black pepper

Combine the garlic, rosemary, parsley, lemon zest, grated Parmesan and a little salt and pepper in a bowl, then place this mixture around the cavity of the pork, pressing it in well. Tie up with kitchen string so the filling doesn't escape.

Heat 2 tablespoons of olive oil in a large saucepan over a medium-to-high heat, add the pork and seal well on all sides for about 20 minutes, then add the wine and allow it to evaporate. Transfer the pork to a plate and set aside.

Heat the remaining olive oil in the same pan, add the onion, celery and carrot and sweat over a medium heat for about 5 minutes until softened. Return the pork to the pan, then add the tomato passata and enough water to nearly cover the pork. Bring to the boil, then reduce the heat, partially cover with a lid and cook gently for 3½ hours until the meat is tender and almost falling off the bone and the tomato sauce has thickened.

Remove the pork and slice the meat, then serve with a little of the tomato sauce. You can also serve the tomato sauce with some freshly cooked pasta, if you like.

POLENTA CON COSTINE DI MAIALE

Polenta with spare ribs

I love spare ribs, especially when slow-cooked in a tomato sauce and the meat is literally hanging off the bone. They are delicious served on top of runny polenta and this makes a hearty meal.

In Italy, especially in rural areas, polenta dishes like this are typically served on a large wooden board placed in the centre of the table and everyone digs in with their fork without the need to have individual plates. Not everyone might agree for hygiene purposes these days, but it's a lovely rustic way to serve this dish and saves on washing up, too!

Serves 4

3 tbsp extra virgin olive oil
800g (1lb 12oz) pork spare ribs
½ onion, finely chopped
1 celery stick, finely chopped
1 small carrot, finely chopped
2 bay leaves

70ml (2½fl oz) white wine
2 x 400g (14oz) cans chopped tomatoes
2 tsp tomato purée, mixed with a little water
800ml (28fl oz) water or vegetable stock
200g (7oz) quick-cook polenta
sea salt

Heat the olive oil in a large saucepan, add the spare ribs and stir-fry over a medium heat until sealed all over, about 10 minutes. Add the onion, celery, carrot and bay leaves and sweat over a medium heat for a couple of minutes. Increase the heat, add the wine and allow it to evaporate.

Add the tomatoes, then rinse out one of the cans with some water (about half a can) and add this along with the tomato purée and some salt. Cover with a lid and cook over a low heat for 1¾ hours until the meat is cooked through.

Just before the end of the cooking time, make the polenta. Pour the water or vegetable stock into a saucepan, bring to the boil, then gradually whisk in the polenta, mixing well to avoid lumps forming, then cook, stirring, for about 3–5 minutes or according to the timing given on the packet.

Immediately pour the polenta onto a wooden board or large plate and then top with the ribs and tomato sauce. Serve immediately.

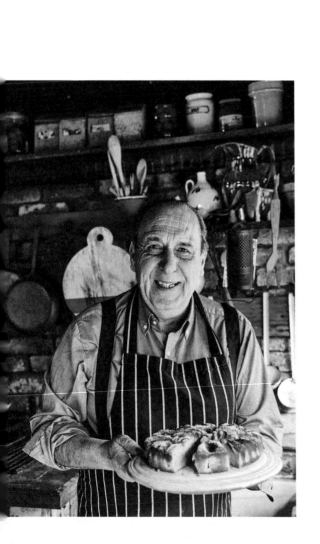

SWEET TREATS

TORTA DI PANE AL CIOCCOLATO

Chocolate bread cake

Bread cakes are one of the best ways to use up leftover stale bread, and in Italy this type of cake is traditional in the Piemonte region. There are many variations, but the one thing they have in common is stale bread soaked in milk and combined with whatever ingredients you have to hand, like dried fruit, fresh fruit, chocolate, nuts or even savoury ingredients. It's a very substantial cake and a slice will keep you going for a while!

Serves 12

300g (10½oz) crustless stale bread
zest and juice of 1 orange
700ml (1¼ pints) hot (not boiling) milk
70g (2½oz) sultanas
120g (4¼oz) crunchy amaretti biscuits, plus
  a few (optional) extra to decorate

a little butter or olive oil, for greasing
50g (1¾oz) cocoa powder, sifted
2 eggs, lightly beaten
120g (4¼oz) caster sugar
30g (1oz) walnuts, roughly chopped

Roughly chop the bread into small pieces, place in a bowl and combine with the orange zest, then stir in the hot milk, cover and leave to soak for 30 minutes until the milk has been absorbed.

In the meantime, soak the sultanas in the orange juice and crush the amaretti biscuits until very fine.

Preheat the oven to 160°C fan/180°C/gas mark 4. Grease a 24cm (9½in.) round springform cake tin and line it with baking paper.

Combine the soaked bread with the crushed amaretti biscuits, the cocoa powder, eggs, sugar, walnuts and the drained sultanas (discard any remaining orange juice). Pour the mixture evenly into the prepared tin, then bake in the oven for about 1 hour or until risen. If you insert a wooden skewer, it should come out clean. The cake is moist so the skewer won't be dry, but should not have gooey cake mixture.

Remove from the oven, then leave to cool completely before carefully removing it from the tin. Place on a plate and decorate with a few whole amaretti biscuits, if desired.

This cake is best eaten fresh but will keep in an airtight container at room temperature for up to 3 days.

TORTA DI MELE

Apple cake

This rustic apple cake is so simple to make and the result is wonderfully soft. I'm sure it will become a family favourite. I highly recommend the Italian sachets of baking powder (*Paneangeli*) that are available from Italian delis as this not only adds a wonderful softness to the cake but it has a wonderful aroma of vanilla. Of course, normal baking powder will work, too. Enjoy a slice with coffee or tea or as a dessert, perhaps with some mascarpone, cream or custard.

Serves 8

3 eating apples, any type you have at home
zest and juice of 1 lemon
150g (5½oz) caster sugar
2 large eggs
1 tsp vanilla extract
50ml (2fl oz) sunflower or vegetable oil, plus
*   extra for greasing*

200g (7oz) plain flour, sifted
1 x 16g (½oz) sachet Paneangeli baking
*   powder, sifted, or use 16g (½oz) regular*
*   baking powder*
200ml (7fl oz) natural yogurt
2 tsp icing sugar
1 tsp ground cinnamon

Preheat the oven to 160°C fan/180°C/gas mark 4. Lightly grease a 24cm (9½in.) loose-bottomed round cake tin.

Peel and remove the cores from the apples, then cut into thin slices and leave in acidulated water (mix the lemon juice with some cold water in a bowl).

Place the sugar, eggs, vanilla and lemon zest in a mixing bowl and, using an electric whisk, whisk for about 5 minutes until nice and creamy and pale in colour. Whisk in the oil. Fold in the flour, baking powder and yogurt until well combined. Pour the mixture evenly into the prepared cake tin.

Drain the apples well and dry on kitchen paper, then arrange the slices over the top of the cake. Combine the icing sugar and cinnamon and lightly sprinkle all over the apples.

Bake in the oven for about 45–50 minutes or until golden brown and risen.

Remove from the oven, then leave to cool completely in the tin. Carefully remove the cake from the tin and serve in slices.

This cake is best eaten fresh but will keep in an airtight container at room temperature for up to 2 days.

SCARPACCIA VIAREGGINA

Courgette tart

This 'poor man's' sweet tart has ancient origins and is a popular dessert during the spring/summer when courgettes are plentiful, tender and sweet in the Tuscan seaside town of Viareggio. The name *Scarpaccia*, meaning 'old shoe', probably comes from the fact that this custard-like dessert is as flat as an old shoe. In fact, when it comes out of the oven it almost looks like a baked omelette. If you are making it out of season or can't get the small courgettes, then regular courgettes will be just fine.

Serves 4–6

1 egg
85g (3oz) caster sugar
25g (1oz) butter, melted
1 tsp vanilla extract
65ml (2¼fl oz) milk
zest of 1 small lemon, plus (optional) extra zest to decorate
75g (2¾oz) plain flour, sifted
4g (⅛oz) baking powder, sifted
250g (9oz) small or baby courgettes, very finely sliced
extra virgin olive oil, for drizzling, plus a little extra for the tin

Preheat the oven to 180°C fan/200°C/gas mark 6. Grease and line a 22cm (8½in.) round sponge cake tin and line it with baking paper.

Whisk the egg and sugar together in a bowl until creamy and pale, then add the melted butter, vanilla extract, milk and lemon zest. Fold in the flour and baking powder, followed by the courgettes. Pour the mixture evenly into the prepared cake tin and drizzle with a little olive oil.

Bake in the oven for 5 minutes, then reduce the oven temperature to 160°C fan/180°C/gas mark 4 and continue to bake for a further 50 minutes until a golden brown crust appears on top.

Remove from the oven and leave to cool completely in the tin. Carefully remove the tart from the tin, then slice and serve sprinkled with a little lemon zest, if desired.

This tart is best eaten fresh on the day, or the next.

MIGLIACCIO NAPOLETANO

Neapolitan semolina cake

This ancient Neapolitan cake-like dessert was traditionally made with millet, a popular staple grain of the *cucina povera*. To enrich it further, pig's blood was added to the mixture, but this tradition has long ceased. Nowadays, semolina is used to prepare this sweet treat, which is usually eaten during *Carnevale*, and with the addition of ricotta and the aroma of vanilla and citrus, it encompasses the flavours of this southern Italian region perfectly.

Serves 8

500ml (18fl oz) milk
500ml (18fl oz) water
a little pared rind of 1 lemon and 1 orange
  (rest of zest is also used – see opposite)
40g (1½oz) butter, plus extra for greasing
200g (7oz) semolina flour
4 eggs

250g (9oz) caster sugar
2 tsp vanilla extract
zest of 1 lemon and 1 orange (taken from
  the same fruit as the pared rinds)
250g (9oz) ricotta, drained
icing sugar, for sprinkling

Preheat the oven to 180°C fan/200°C/gas mark 6. Lightly grease a 24cm (9½in.) loose-bottomed round cake tin with butter and line it with baking paper.

Combine the milk, water, pared citrus rinds and butter in a large saucepan and cook over a low-medium heat until the butter has melted. Increase the heat and bring to the boil, discard the citrus rinds, then gradually whisk in the semolina and continue to cook and whisk over a medium heat for about 4 minutes until the mixture thickens. Remove from the heat and pour onto a large plate to cool.

In the meantime, place the eggs, caster sugar and vanilla in a mixing bowl and, using an electric whisk, whisk together for about 5 minutes until nice and creamy. Add the citrus zests, then gradually add the ricotta and the semolina mixture, whisking until well incorporated.

Pour evenly into the prepared cake tin, then bake in the oven for about 1 hour, until golden brown. If, after 40 minutes or so, you find the top is getting too brown, cover with a piece of foil and continue to bake.

Remove from the oven, then leave to cool completely in the tin. Carefully remove the cake from the tin. Sprinkle with some sifted icing sugar and serve

This cake will keep in an airtight container at room temperature for up to 3 days.

SBRICIOLONA DI PESCHE

Peach crumble cake

A crumble cake in Italy is tied to peasant roots and is a typical sweet of the Mantova region in northern Italy. The original *Sbrisolona*, as it is known in the local dialect, meaning 'breadcrumbs', was made with local ingredients of hazelnuts and polenta flour and no sugar. Over time, this recipe has evolved and although it is still made with nuts, creamy fillings such as chocolate spread or ricotta are used as well as fruit. This version is made with canned peaches, which are easily obtainable all year round and an easy storecupboard ingredient, but in season you can use fresh peaches, if you prefer. You could substitute the peaches with other fruit, such as apricots, pears or apples. This cake is delicious served with whipped ricotta on the side, if desired.

Serves 8

500g (1lb 2oz) canned or fresh peaches
300g (10½oz) plain flour, plus extra
  for dusting
8g (⅓oz) (½ sachet) Paneangeli baking
  powder, or use 8g (⅓oz) regular
  baking powder
100g (3½oz) caster sugar

100g (3½oz) chilled butter, cut into small
  pieces, plus extra for greasing
1 egg, lightly beaten
250g (9oz) ricotta, drained
2 tbsp icing sugar, sifted
2 tsp vanilla extract

Preheat the oven to 170°C fan/190°C/gas mark 5. Grease a 24cm (9½in.) round springform cake tin with butter, then dust with flour, tapping out the excess.

Drain the peaches well and then cut into slices. Discard the stones before slicing, if using fresh peaches. Set aside.

Sift the flour and baking powder into a mixing bowl, stir in the caster sugar, then rub in the butter until the mixture resembles fine breadcrumbs. Gradually add the egg and gently mix with your fingertips until the egg is incorporated to make a crumble mixture.

Place two-thirds of the crumble mix in the prepared tin, gently spreading it out evenly to the edges. Arrange the peach slices over the top, leaving about a 1cm (½in.) border free around the edge, then cover with the remaining crumble mix, filling in the gaps to cover the fruit.

Bake in the oven for about 40 minutes until golden. Remove from the oven, then leave to rest for 5 minutes before carefully removing the cake from the tin and placing it on a serving plate.

While the baked cake is resting, whip the ricotta with the icing sugar and vanilla in a bowl until light and fluffy. Slice the crumble cake and serve warm or cold with the whipped ricotta.

This cake is best eaten on the day it is made, but it will keep in an airtight container in the fridge for up to 2 days. The whipped ricotta will keep in a covered container in the fridge for up to 2 days.

PASTICCINI DI CASTAGNE

Sweet chestnut pastries

Believe it or not, chestnuts were once food of the poor and very much part of *cucina povera*. In season, we always had chestnuts in Italy and lots of dishes, both sweet and savoury, were made. Chestnuts were also ground into flour and made into pasta, bread and cakes. These pastries are popular in the pastry shops of my hometown of Minori on the Amalfi Coast and, because I love chestnuts so much, I had to include them in this book. They take a little time to make, but really are well worth the effort.

Makes 12 pastries

For the chestnuts
300g (10½oz) fresh raw chestnuts
1 tsp sea salt
1 bay leaf
1 tsp fennel seeds
1 tbsp caster sugar

For the pastry
250g (9oz) plain flour, plus extra for dusting
pinch of sea salt
125g (4½oz) hard butter, cut into
  small pieces
100g (3½oz) caster sugar

zest of 1 small lemon
2 egg yolks

For the filling
40g (1½oz) caster sugar
1 tsp vanilla extract
20g (¾oz) cocoa powder, sifted
2 tsp raisins, soaked in 1 tbsp rum
150ml (5fl oz) milk, plus extra for brushing

icing sugar, sifted to decorate (optional)

First make the pastry. Combine the flour and salt in a large bowl, add the butter and rub together with your fingertips until it resembles breadcrumbs. Stir in the sugar and lemon zest then gradually add the egg yolks, mixing with your hands until you obtain a smooth dough – if necessary add a little cold water. Form into a ball, wrap in parchment paper and leave to rest in the fridge.

In the meantime, cook the chestnuts. Place all the ingredients in a pan, cover with water, place over the heat, bring to the boil, then simmer for about 30 minutes until the chestnuts are cooked through. Depending on size, you may need more or less cooking time.

Drain the chestnuts, cool slightly, then peel and remove the internal skin. While still warm, mash the chestnuts – I find this easier with a potato ricer.

Now make the filling. Place the mashed chestnuts in a saucepan, add the sugar and combine. Stir in the vanilla, cocoa powder and raisins, together with the rum, then gradually whisk in the milk, ensuring there are no lumps. Cook over a medium heat for about 15 minutes, stirring with a whisk or wooden spoon, until the milk is absorbed and you have a thick, creamy consistency. Remove from the heat and set aside to cool.

Preheat the oven to 160°C fan/180°C/gas mark 4. Line a baking sheet with baking paper.

Roll out the pastry on a lightly floured surface to about 5mm (¼in.) thickness. Cut out 10 circles using a 8cm (3¼in.) round pastry cutter and then cut out 10 more circles using a 7cm (2¾in.) round pastry cutter, re-rolling the trimmings, if needed.

Place a dollop of the filling in the centre of each of the larger pastry circles, then place a smaller pastry circle on top of each, then press and crimp all around the edges to seal. Place in a muffin tin, brush the tops with a little milk and bake in the oven for 25–30 minutes until golden brown.

Remove from the oven, cool slightly, then serve with a sprinkling of sifted icing sugar, if desired. If serving cold, these pastries will keep in an airtight container at room temperature for up to 3 days.

SEADAS

Sardinian sweet ravioli

These sweet fried ravioli-type pastries originate from the Sardinian *cucina povera,* using the local ingredients of leftover pasta dough, local cheese and honey. The result is a fantastic combination of savoury and sweet and has become quite a delicacy on the island. Larger than ravioli, serve one per person, immediately after cooking so you taste the warm oozing cheese. For best results, use a young, soft pecorino, obtainable from Italian delis.

6 servings
150g (5½oz) '00' pasta flour
pinch of sea salt
35g (1¼oz) lard
approx. 80ml (2½fl oz) lukewarm water
120g (4¼oz) soft pecorino cheese
zest of 1 orange, plus a little extra to serve
abundant vegetable oil, for frying
runny honey, for drizzling

Combine the flour, salt and lard in a bowl, then gradually add enough lukewarm water to make a smooth dough. Tip onto the work surface, then knead the dough for 5 minutes until soft and pliable. Wrap in clingfilm and leave to rest for 30 minutes at room temperature.

In the meantime, grate the pecorino and combine with the orange zest in a bowl.

Roll out the dough as thinly as you can on a lightly floured surface; if you use a pasta machine, roll it on the thinnest setting.

Cut out twelve circles using a 10cm (4in.) round pastry or biscuit cutter. With your hands, place a walnut-sized amount of filling in the centre of six of the dough circles, then place the remaining dough circles over the top and press the edges together well to seal.

Heat plenty of oil in a deep frying pan until hot. Add a few *seadas* and shallow-fry over a medium-to-high heat until golden all over, about 5 minutes – if you prefer not to flip them, simply spoon hot oil over the top. Remove and drain on kitchen paper. Keep warm while you fry the remaining *seadas* in the same way.

Place the hot *seadas* on serving plates, drizzle over some honey, sprinkle with a little extra orange zest and serve immediately.

MELANZANE ALLA CIOCCOLATA

Chocolate aubergines

This is quite an old traditional recipe and there are many stories of how this unusual dessert came about. Some say it was invented by nuns, from the convent who made a similar dish for the birth of the grandson of a Russian Tzar visiting the Amalfi Coast; or Franciscan monks who would drizzle aubergines with their homemade sweet liqueur; or more recently, during WW2 when the Americans arrived and gave jars of chocolate to the farmers who used it to make a dish like this one. Whichever story is correct, these sweet treats are enjoyed during the *Ferragosto* holiday along the Amalfi and Sorrento Coasts. This is my sister, Adriana's, version and I love it!

Serves 12

100g (3½oz) cocoa powder (minimum 70%), sifted
50g (1¾oz) plain flour, plus extra
* for dusting*
400g (14oz) caster sugar
550ml (19fl oz) water
200g (7oz) dark chocolate, broken up into small pieces
50ml (2fl oz) Vin Santo, Marsala or Amaretto
3 aubergines, peeled and thinly sliced
abundant vegetable oil, for frying
4 eggs, beaten
16 amaretti biscuits, crushed
ground cinnamon, for dusting (optional)
zest of 1 lemon
zest of 1 orange
handful of flaked almonds

Combine the cocoa powder and flour in a bowl and gradually whisk in 300ml (10fl oz) of water, ensuring no lumps. Set aside.

Place the sugar and 250ml (9fl oz) of water in a saucepan over a medium heat, stirring all the time to dissolve the sugar. Once dissolved, continue to stir over the heat for a couple of minutes. Remove from the heat, add the chocolate pieces; mixing until the chocolate has melted.

Gradually add the chocolate mixture to the cocoa mixture, whisking well to prevent lumps forming. Return to the heat, stir in the liquor and cook over a medium heat, stirring all the time, for 5 minutes until you obtain a silky, smooth consistency. Remove from the heat and set aside.

Heat plenty of vegetable oil in a deep frying pan until hot, add the aubergine slices and deep-fry for a couple of minutes until golden on each side. Remove and drain well on kitchen paper.

Coat the fried aubergine slices in flour, then dip in the egg. Heat plenty of clean oil in a deep frying pan, then fry the eggy aubergine slices until golden on each side, about 1–2 minutes. Remove and drain well on kitchen paper.

Line a pyrex-type dish, approximately 5cm (2in.) in depth, with a little of the chocolate sauce. Dip the aubergine slices in the bowl of chocolate and then create a layer in the bottom of the dish. Scatter some crushed amaretti biscuits over the top, followed by a pinch of cinnamon (if using) and a little of the citrus zests. Make another layer in the same way. Top with the remaining crushed amaretti biscuits, cinnamon (if using), citrus zests and the flaked almonds.

Cover and store in the fridge until required. This dessert will keep in the fridge for up to 5 days.

FRITTELLE DI RICOTTA

Mini ricotta doughnuts

Sweet doughnuts were traditionally eaten in Italy during *Carnevale* – the period just before Lent starts – as a way of feasting on sweet, indulgent food before the holy period, when sweets were forbidden. Over time, this has changed, but doughnuts are still popular during *Carnevale* and other festivities and each region has its favourites. These wonderfully light, fluffy mini doughnuts probably came about as a way of using up leftover ricotta in households where this soft cheese was widely used in everyday cooking. These are simply flavoured with vanilla, but you could also add lemon or orange zest. Give them a go, you won't regret it and, once you start to eat them, you'll find it's really difficult to stop!

Makes about 40 mini doughnuts
2 eggs
250g (9oz) ricotta, drained
50g (1¾oz) caster sugar, plus extra for rolling
100g (3½oz) plain flour or '00' pasta flour, sifted
8g (⅓oz) (½ a sachet) Paneangeli baking powder, or use
  8g (⅓oz) regular baking powder
1 tsp vanilla extract
abundant vegetable or sunflower oil, for deep-frying

In a bowl, beat the eggs with a fork, then add the ricotta and continue to beat until well incorporated. Beat in the sugar, flour, sifted baking powder and the vanilla.

Heat plenty of oil in a pan suitable for deep-frying until hot, then add teaspoonfuls of the mixture and deep-fry for a couple of minutes until golden. You will have to work in batches and keep an eye on the oil; if you find the doughnuts get brown too quickly, reduce the heat. The doughnuts need to be golden on the outside and cooked and fluffy on the inside.

Remove and drain using a slotted spoon, then place each batch on kitchen paper to absorb the excess oil. Repeat to make the remaining doughnuts (you'll make about 40 in total).

Place a little caster sugar in a dish and toss the cooked doughnuts in the sugar to coat. These are delicious served warm.

ROTOLO DOLCE DI ZUCCA

Sweet pumpkin roll

Although not a traditional dessert from the *cucina povera*, pumpkin was certainly an ingredient that was widely used in rural areas during the autumn. It was cooked in many different savoury dishes, but because of its sweetness, I like adding it to desserts. The sweetness of puréed pumpkin, with a hint of cinnamon combines really well with the whipped ricotta filling. To save time, you can buy cans of ready-puréed pumpkin.

Serves 8

For the sponge
approx. 850g (1lb 14oz) unprepped pumpkin
 (to make 150g/5½oz of purée)
a little butter or olive oil, for greasing
3 eggs
150g (5½oz) caster sugar, plus extra
 for sprinkling
1 tsp vanilla extract
100g (3½oz) plain flour
1 tsp baking powder
2 tsp ground cinnamon

For the filling
400g (14oz) ricotta, well drained
100g (3½oz) icing sugar, sifted, plus extra
 for dusting
zest of 1 orange – use orange segments
 to decorate
30g (1oz) chocolate chips, milk or dark

Swiss roll baking tray 38cm x 25cm
 (15 x 10in.), lightly greased with butter
 and lined with parchment paper

Preheat the oven to 180°C fan/200°C/gas mark 6.

First make the pumpkin purée. Cut the pumpkin into thin slices, remove the seeds, then place the slices on a large baking sheet and roast in the oven for about 25 minutes until softened. Remove from the oven, leave to cool, then remove the flesh from the skin, place in a blender or food processor and blend until smooth and creamy. Weigh the purée – you should have 150g (5½oz). Set aside.

Reduce the oven temperature 160°C fan/180°C/gas mark 4. Lightly grease a baking tray or Swiss roll tin with a little butter or olive oil, then line with baking paper.

To make the sponge, use an electric whisk to whisk the eggs and sugar together in a mixing bowl for about 5 minutes until creamy and pale. Whisk in the vanilla and pumpkin purée. Sift in the flour, baking powder and cinnamon and gently fold in until combined. Pour onto the baking tray or Swiss roll tin, gently spread it out evenly, then bake in the oven for 15 minutes until risen and golden.

In the meantime, prepare a sheet of baking paper on the work surface and sprinkle with a little caster sugar. Turn the baked sponge out onto the sugared paper and carefully peel off

the lining paper, then gently roll up the sponge from the longer edge, using the paper to help you. Leave to cool.

To make the filling, place the ricotta in a bowl, sift in the icing sugar, add the orange zest and chocolate chips and stir until combined.

Carefully unroll the cold sponge, spread the filling evenly all over, then re-roll without the sugared paper. Dust with icing sugar and decorate with orange segments. Serve in slices.

This cake is best eaten on the day it is made, but it will keep in an airtight container in the fridge for up to 2 days.

BISCOTTI DA INZUPPO

Old-fashioned dunking biscuits

I remember growing up with biscuits like these, which we would often have for breakfast and mid-afternoon to dunk into bowls of warm milk or *caffé latte* (milky coffee). Biscuits like these would normally be made at home, perhaps once a week, and kept in an airtight tin; you only needed one biscuit to dunk as they were extremely tasty and filling and were a great way to start the day. While testing the recipe for this book, they really took me back to my childhood days and I couldn't wait to enjoy one with a milky coffee.

Makes 15

1 x 16g (½oz) sachet of Paneangeli baking powder, or use 16g (½oz) regular baking powder

60ml (2¼fl oz) lukewarm milk

180g (6½oz) caster sugar, plus extra for sprinkling

2 eggs

pinch of sea salt

zest of 1 lemon

80ml (2½fl oz) olive oil

550g (1lb 4oz) plain flour or '00' pasta flour, sifted

Preheat the oven to 160°C fan/180°C/gas mark 4. Line a large baking sheet with baking paper.

Stir the baking powder into the warm milk and set aside.

In a large bowl, whisk together the sugar and eggs for about 5 minutes until creamy. Stir in the salt, lemon zest and olive oil, then gradually fold in the sifted flour and the baking powder/milk mixture. Mix together well to make a soft dough, then tip onto the work surface and knead for 10 minutes.

Shape the dough into a 1metre (40in.) long sausage, approx. 4cm (1½in.) wide, then cut into approx. 6.5cm (2½in.) lengths. You should end up with 15 pieces. With your hands, flatten and lengthen each piece slightly, rounding off the ends.

Place the shaped pieces of dough on the prepared baking sheet, sprinkle with a little caster sugar and then bake in the oven for 20 minutes until lightly golden. Remove from the oven, leave to cool completely on the baking sheet, then serve cold.

These biscuits will keep in an airtight container at room temperature for up to a week (if they last that long!).

INDEX

ACKNOWLEDEGMENTS

Liz Przybylski for writing and organising.

Adriana Contaldo for recipe testing and cooking
at the shoots.

David Loftus for fantastic photography throughout.

Pip Spence for beautiful food and prop styling on set.

Laura Russell for all her design work.

Ellen Simmons for guiding us throughout the whole process
and washing up during the shoots!

Sophie Allen, Cara Armstrong, Stephanie Milner at Pavilion.

Pavilion
An imprint of HarperCollinsPublishers Ltd
1 London Bridge Street
London SE1 9GF

www.harpercollins.co.uk

HarperCollinsPublishers
Macken House, 39/40 Mayor Street Upper
Dublin 1, D01 C9W8
Ireland

10 9 8 7 6 5 4 3 2

First published in Great Britain by
Pavilion, an imprint of HarperCollinsPublishers
Ltd 2022

Text © Gennaro Contaldo 2022

Gennaro Contaldo asserts the moral right to be
identified as the author of this work.
A catalogue record for this book is available from
the British Library.

ISBN 978-1-911682-60-8

This book is produced from independently
certified FSC™ paper to ensure responsible
forest management.

For more information visit:
www.harpercollins.co.uk/green

Printed and bound in Bosnia and Herzegovina by GPS Group

Photography: David Loftus
Layout: Kei Ishimaru
Design Manager: Laura Russell
Food Stylist: Pip Spence
Editor: Cara Armstrong, Ellen Simmons